from The Garden

GREAT VEGETABLE COOKING
FROM MARKET TO TABLE

Judy Schultz

Paintings by Vivian Thierfelder

Red Deer College Press

The Publishers
Red Deer College Press
56 Avenue & 32 Street Box 5005 Red Deer Alberta Canada T4N 5H5

Design and Typography by Boldface Technologies Inc.
Printed and Bound in Singapore by Kyodo Printing Co. Pte. Ltd.

Special thanks to Patricia Roy for her assistance in the preparation of this book.

Financial support provided by the Alberta Foundation for the Arts, a beneficiary of the Lottery Fund of the Government of Alberta, and by the Department of Communications and Red Deer College.

Canadian Cataloguing in Publication Data
Schultz, Judy
From the garden
ISBN 0-88995-104-7
1. Cookery (Vegetables). 2. Vegetable gardening. I. Title.
TX801.S38 1993 641.6'5 C93-091493-7

from the Garden

Great Vegetable Cooking
from Market to Table

Judy Schultz

for Eddie

This book could not have been written without the help of those people who really understand vegetables· producers, marketers, and cooks who work with vegetables every day.

For always being just a phone call away, whether in the field, the market, the kitchen, or smack in the middle of a meeting, I thank the bean lady, Vi Bretin of Bioway Gardens; the tomato-and-corn women, Lois and Valerie Hole of Hole's Greenhouse; the foragers, Rita and Otto Holzbauer of Mo-Na Mushrooms; the marketing whiz, Gabe Keller of The Grocery People; the amazing Smoky Lake Pumpkin Growers; and the vegetable growers of the Old Strathcona Farmers Market and the Edmonton City Market.

For sharing recipes and methods with me, I thank Paula Wiel, Janos Theopolis, Vi Bretin, Susan Toy, Larry Stewart, Brian Green, Maureen Hemingway, Ba Ng Tranh, Marcine Hunt, Bobby Wong, and many other good cooks who have been so generous with their special knowledge.

I'm also grateful to my fellow food scribes across the country whose work has delighted, encouraged, and inspired me for so long: Rose Murray, Monda Rosenberg, Carol Ferguson, Noel Richardson, Elizabeth Baird, James Barber, and the late Mme Jehane Benoit who inspired us all.

I thank my publisher, Dennis Johnson, for his unswerving enthusiasm and sense of humor; Patricia Roy, for her patient and careful editing; and Vivian Thierfelder, for her stunning watercolor paintings.

from The Garden

Contents

Contents

From The Garden

Contents

The Love of Vegetables

POPULAR MYTHOLOGY HAS IT THAT children naturally despise vegetables. From the beginning, I didn't conform to the myth. I grew up in an extended family that devoted a lot of energy to the quality of life around the table. The cooks – my mother, resident grandmother, and a variety of visiting aunts – were all gardening cooks. It wasn't a big deal; it was simply the way they lived. Their unabashed awe at the first radish of spring, and their delight as the new potatoes were scratched out of the side of a hill or the last cabbage was harvested, taught me something about living well. My years in those sociable kitchens, while the women planted and harvested, pickled and stewed, cooked, tasted, and endlessly discussed, were good times.

Without knowing it, Mom and Grandma were sensualists. Their pleasure in the burnished orange of a pumpkin or the warm licorice smell of fresh dill was nothing short of erotic.

If you asked, they could describe their garden pleasures exactly, so you knew that particular shade of red the sun lends to a tomato in late August and the dusty sweet smell when you pinch out the sucker leaves or break the fruit from the stem. They could even describe the sound inside your own head when your teeth bite into a tomato because eating is not a silent act – it's loud and slurpy, or at least it should be, if the tomato is properly, juicily ripe.

Knowing all that, you'd understand the flavor of vegetables as they should be, fresh and simple, and you'd have what Mom called standards.

I still love the luminous colors, the textures, the smells of earth and new growth that garden vegetables bring to the kitchen. Apart from everything else, they are reminders of the changing seasons.

Not That Plastic Junk . . .

In the last years of her life, when her world had shrunk to the length and breadth of her hospital room, my mother still enjoyed good food, especially the fresh vegetables she used to grow.

Sundays, I took lunch to the hospital. But first, there was a long phone call while she decided what she wanted to eat. Often it would be a baked potato, with a side order of green onions and little radishes. "Not the big woody ones! If they're woody, forget it. . . ."

In summer, lunch might revolve around a ripe tomato. "Garden-ripe," she'd say. "Not that plastic junk. . . ."

She'd have turned her nose up at pâté de foie gras, but give her a dish of fresh green peas and she was content. She longed for the honest flavors and textures of a happier time, when she had her own garden and ran her own kitchen. For Mom, food evoked the strongest memories, the best memories, and gave her pleasure when she needed it most.

Different Garden, Same Feeling

My mother, my grandmothers, and all those wonderful aunts taught me an abiding respect for the earth and its gifts, each in its season, and I grew up cranky about the way chefs treated vegetables and the way major commercial producers sacrificed quality for quantity.

When I began making a living as a food writer and restaurant critic, I was temporarily without my own garden patch. But, constant prowling for better sources introduced me to the army of gardeners who supplied local farmers markets.

Gradually, I began searching for the roots of our major cuisines, wandering hungrily through the old world markets of Europe and North Africa, China and Southeast Asia. To my prairie eyes, the vegetables seemed strange and exotic, but the growers and cooks were not very different from those I'd grown up with. Through their gardens, markets, and kitchens, they let me touch their own roots.

True, they disagreed wildly on many points. The French served vegetables nearly raw; the Italians cooked them until they were squishy. The French ate salad after the meal; the Italians liked it with. And so forth. But underneath, they had something in common – they all knew that the best tomato was the one they grew in their own garden.

Today I live in a city with two year-round farmers markets, in a rich agricultural area where many gardeners have shared their knowledge with me.

I'm a cook, not an expert gardener. My basil usually succumbs to bugs before I can harvest a major crop, but I grow it anyway, for its clovey-grassy-lemony smell, as long as it lasts. I love my overgrown mint patch, perfuming the air when Ed mows over it, perfuming the dogs when they roll in it. Should it decide to turn up its toes next season, I'll mourn it briefly and start again because gardening cooks are eternal optimists.

What About Meat?

I eat my share. This is not a vegetarian cookbook. Rather, it's a book about the pleasures of vegetables, and meat is used, although sparingly, and often as a flavor enhancer. Bacon, prosciutto, a bit of well-made sausage adds oomph to many dishes, especially

from The Garden

winter dishes where a little meat lends a vital cushion of heft and flavor, a smoky, buttery undertone. Somehow, it reminds us of ancestral fires in long-forgotten hearths.

Nailing Down Your Sources

To enjoy cooking and eating vegetables, you must have them as soon as possible from the garden. Ignore those poor, juiceless tomatoes and that long-ago picked corn.

Find your own grower. He's out there, in the pick-your-own garden, the farmgate stand, the farmers market. Take him to lunch, bring him chocolates, offer him dibs on your Hawaiian time-share. Cultivate this more-than-passing acquaintance as you would a banker who could loan you Porsche money at prime rate.

Freshness is one thing. Variety is another. Buyers for chain supermarkets are not inclined to waste their efforts on tiny garden gems with short seasons, skin too delicate to be machine-harvested, and a brief shelf life. In fact, unless a tomato has the keeping qualities of a tennis ball, it likely won't make it to your local supermarket.

By contrast, farmers markets are full of dedicated vegetable growers who trial five or six varieties of corn or tomatoes every year, or plant unusual seeds on spec. Horticultural oddities pique the curiosity of the genuine gardener, and you might be the only urbanite who gets to enjoy them, if only for a single season.

The Best Ingredient

Long ago, in her Bologna kitchen, Marcella Hazan gave me a piece of advice that has ever since served me well with gardens, markets, and other people's recipes: "The best ingredient in the kitchen is common sense." I can't improve on that.

This is not intended to be an encyclopedia. The recipes in this book all reflect the personal taste of one individual – me.

In testing the recipes, the vegetables I used were grown in different soils, climates, and seasons than those you may encounter, so they may have had more (or less) juice, their skin may have been thicker (or thinner), their flavor more (or less) intense. That's why these recipes should be your guide rather than your formula. In the end, they have to please one individual – you.

Part 1: Flavorings

Oils

I'M DELIGHTED WITH THE RANGE OF OILS THAT I'M ONLY NOW discovering: walnut, avocado, hazelnut, grape seed, pumpkin seed, almond, mustard – and these are just the beginning.

The intrepid cook can stock an entire pantry with exotic oils in pretty bottles, but the investment will be considerable and the dividend questionable. If you use the oil only once, it's a wasted investment.

Instead, choose three or four basic oils, experiment with them, and find the ones whose flavors and textures suit you best. They'll add dimension to vegetable dishes, especially salads and breads. Here's what I use:

■ *Canola oil:* The bland, pale, straw-colored oil of the rapeseed has no discernible flavor, a high smoke point, and is extremely low in saturated fats. It's also inexpensive. The potentially troublesome erucic acid that was once present in rapeseed oil has been almost entirely bred out of contemporary varieties of the seed. All in all, canola is an excellent all-purpose oil for salads, for deep-frying, and for infusing with other flavors such as herbs or garlic.

■ *Extra-virgin olive oil:* What you have here is fruit juice – the juice of the olive, pressed without heat or the addition of chemicals, and with its color, flavor, and aroma intact. In the premium olive oils, the personal taste of the grower/producer will be obvious. So will several other factors relating to where it was grown, the climate during the growing season, and how the olives were treated during harvest. Were they picked and processed quickly, at peak quality? Or were they carelessly handled, bashed, bruised, allowed to languish in nets or bins and to ferment before they reached the press?

There are as many variations as there are producers, and one is not necessarily better than another. Your personal taste is the only one that counts now.

Extra-virgin olive oil will cost much more than the same amount of bland commercial olive oil that has been chemically corrected. But remember, the flavor of the fruit is what you're paying for. Buy it in small quantities and keep it in a cool, dark place. If you're really in the chips, buy a second bottle and infuse it with a good bash of garlic. It will be wonderful for salads and stir-fries.

■ *Sesame oil:* The smoky flavor of toasted sesame oil is essential for many Korean, Japanese, and Chinese dishes. I prefer the Japanese brands for their cleaner, non-burned taste. Buy a small bottle and use it sparingly until you get used to the assertive flavor.

Infused Oils

Infusing a mild oil with herbs and spices of your choice is easy, and the results can be spectacular.

I've found the easiest way is to heat the oil to a simmer, add the flavoring elements, turn the heat off, and let steep in this hot oil bath for a few minutes before bottling. Heating the oil and flavoring elements together gives the infusion a kick-start.

The other, more gradual method is to add the flavoring elements to the clean bottle and pour in the hot oil. This way seems easier, but the infusion takes somewhat longer to develop.

■ *Two cautions:* If you use the first method, do not overheat the oil or you'll burn the seasonings. The result will be bitterly disappointing. (And, disappointingly bitter. Burned garlic is nasty stuff. If it happens, throw it out and start over.) Because this is an infusion, the oil temperature must reach no higher than 225 F (110 C) on a candy thermometer, or a gentle simmer with the oil wiggling nicely. Watch it carefully because it takes only a few seconds for the oil to jump from a gently simmering 225 F (110 C) to a rollicking 350 F (180 C).

The second caution is to work in small batches. Infused oils are highly flavored, so a little goes a long way. There's no point in concocting vats of the stuff until you've tried it and know how much and how often you'll use it. In that way, you can keep a variety of flavored oils on hand with minimal investment.

Lemon Ginger Stir-Fry Oil

The best oil for this infusion is a bland one such as canola. Save your extra-virgin for the pure garlic infusion you'll want for pasta and pesto. This richly aromatic oil is excellent for vegetable stir-fries involving seafood, chicken, or pork, and on the grill it enhances bland vegetables such as eggplant or zucchini. It can also be added to marinades and to salad dressings.

Lemon grass is a favorite ingredient in Thai and Chinese cooking as it adds a subtle lemon ginger perfume to many dishes. In the shops, it looks something like a scrawny leek or an overgrown green onion with an enlarged pale-colored base. Look for fresh lemon grass in oriental shops, and aim for the stalks that have fresh, green leaves on them.

Makes 2 cups (500 mL)

2 cups	canola oil	500 mL
	peel of 1/2 lemon, in strips	
2	lemon grass bulbs, white part only	2
2 inch	piece of peeled fresh ginger	5 cm
4 to 6	cloves garlic, cut in half	4 to 6
6	dried chili peppers	6

In a non-metallic pot, heat oil only until it wiggles.

With a vegetable peeler, remove the peel from half a lemon, keeping it in one long strip, if possible.

☐ Remove the dry outer layer from the lemon grass and discard. Cut off the bulb end and slice it thinly. Slice the ginger diagonally into coins, then mince as fine as possible.

Peel and halve the garlic cloves.

Add the flavoring agents to the hot oil: lemon peel, lemon grass, ginger, garlic, and chili peppers. Immediately turn the heat off, cover the pot, and let the flavorings steep for 15 minutes.

Carefully pour the oil and the flavoring agents into a sterilized, 2 cup (500 mL) jar or bottle and allow to cool. Once cooled, cover tightly and refrigerate. It may cloud but will clear when it comes to room temperature. Use the oil within two months.

Garlic-Infused Olive Oil

In this loud, garlicky infusion, the garlic is not added to the oil. Rather, the garlic cloves, slightly bruised to release the juices, are packed into a clean bottle, and the oil, just at boiling point, is poured over them.

The flavor infuses slowly, gently producing a sweet, aromatic oil that is perfect for pesto, for tossing with spaghetti and grated cheese, for brushing croutons before baking, or for drizzling over focaccia. If possible, the oil you choose for this should have a warm, nutty character. One from Liguria or Tuscany would be a good candidate.

Makes 2 cups (500 mL)

10 to 12	cloves garlic	10 to 12
5 or 6	black peppercorns	5 or 6
2 cups	extra-virgin olive oil	500 mL

☐ Peel the garlic cloves and bruise them slightly with the flat of a knife blade. Drop the garlic into a sterilized bottle that holds a little more than 2 cups (500 mL). Add the peppercorns.

Heat the oil until it barely simmers, then carefully pour into the bottle. Cap, but do not seal. Let the oil stand until cool. Seal or cork the bottle. Let the flavor ripen at least 24 hours before using. It improves on standing. This oil should be refrigerated. It will cloud when cold, but the flavor will remain fresh and lively longer.

Herb-Infused Drizzling Oil

Loving pizza and its many flatbread cousins as I do, I like to have a small cache of herb-infused oil on hand to drizzle over the doughs before baking. It's also a lovely grilling and basting agent, especially for chicken, fish, or almost any vegetable.

Although you can use any fresh herbs that happen to be taking over your garden, I've had the greatest success with a combination of Greek oregano, rosemary, and garlic. Basil alone also makes an astonishingly aromatic oil, perfect as a marinade or a drizzle with ripe tomatoes, fresh mozzarella, or buffala.

Makes 2 cups (500 mL)

1 cup	basil leaves, packed	250 mL
1/2 cup	rosemary sprigs, packed	125 mL
1/2 cup	Greek oregano sprigs, packed	125 mL
1	clove garlic, sliced	1
8 to 10	peppercorns	8 to 10
2 cups	olive or canola oil	500 mL

☐ Pick the herbs early in the morning, before the sun has had a chance to wilt them. Wash herbs thoroughly and pat dry between clean towels, then spread out well and allow them to air-dry for about 15 minutes.

Put all the herbs, garlic, and peppercorns in a clean, 2 cup (500 mL) jar, bruising them slightly to release the oils and packing them in well. Pour the oil into the jar right to the top. Cap tightly and let the mixture rest in a cool, dark place for about 10 days before using.

Vinegars

From the beginning of recorded culinary history, vinegars have been part of the strange alchemy of good cooking and healthy eating. Vinegar has so excited the imaginations of contemporary cooks that some of us have been known to invest in special bottles, barrels, and mother solutions to attempt our own vinegars. It's a labor of love, but one I can do without because it's as unpredictable as making sourdough.

Happily, there are many excellent vinegars available, and infusing them with herbs is less risky and almost as satisfying to the creative cook than starting from scratch. As with oils, you should taste a variety of vinegars and choose the ones you most enjoy using.

The basic vinegar pantry goes like this:

- ■ ***White wine vinegar:*** Buy a good brand with a mellow rather than a sharp flavor. Use it for vinaigrettes and for making your own infused herbal, fruit, or floral vinegars. A small bottle of champagne vinegar is an extra but lovely in any vinaigrette made with shallots.

- ■ ***Red wine vinegar:*** Sauces, marinades, and heartier vinaigrettes require a robust red wine vinegar. Taste several brands until you find the one you like. Then stick with it.

- ■ ***Cider vinegar:*** The mellow, sweet notes of a well-made cider vinegar begin with the apples it's made from and carry through to the pickles, mustard sauces, and chutneys for which you'll use it.

- ■ ***Balsamic vinegar:*** The venerable balsamic vinegars that originate in and around Modena, Italy, are derived from grape juice that has been heated, then allowed to age for years in wooden casks, probably in the grape grower's attic.

As with extra-virgin olive oil, the flavor of genuine balsamic vinegar reflects the personal taste of its maker, and it is usually produced by a wine grower, starting with juice from his own grapes.

Every now and then, a liter or so is drawn off as a gift to a daughter who is marrying, or to a family member about to emigrate and spend the next decades in some uncivilized household where vinegar comes from the local supermarket and there is no generations-old mother solution, no attic with its lineup of little wooden casks.

Other than that, the precious balsamic vinegar is used sparingly.

If you sample its sweet-sour flavor by putting a drop on the tip of your tongue, you'll also learn something about the wood the vinegar-maker used in his cask, the temperature of the attic he kept it in, how long he let it rest there, and even about the history of his family because the mother solution may be a treasure passed down from his ancestors a century or more ago.

# from The Garden

This knowledge will not come cheap, so be prepared to invest heavily in the little flagon, and use it carefully, sprinkled on the first strawberries of the season or over a perfectly grilled steak.

For less money, you can buy a commercially produced balsamic vinegar that will offer you a hint of the original splendor and will be fairly useful in salads and marinades.

■ *Rice vinegar:* The faint touch of sweetness and the pleasant, almost floral aroma of a good rice vinegar improves marinades, works well in rice or couscous salads, and makes a pleasant seasoning for grilled fish. Although I keep both black and white rice vinegar on hand, you'll have more trouble finding a good black one because the acid level is frequently low and the flavor is more like molasses or soy sauce than vinegar. Keep trying until you find one you like. Rice vinegar is essential for many oriental dipping sauces.

Infused Vinegars

Herb-Infused Vinegar

There are two ways to infuse vinegars. The first, which involves pouring cold vinegar over the herbs and letting them steep in a cool, dark place, takes at least a month.

The second method asks only that the vinegar be brought to a simmer before being added to the herbs. The heat releases the flavors and encourages them to develop quickly, and the vinegar can be used within a few days. Be sure you pick the herbs as early as possible, before the sun hits them.

Some people insist that only one herb should be used in an infusion, but I also enjoy a variety of combinations.

Makes 2 cups (500 mL)

1 cup	fresh herbs, picked early	250 mL
2 cups	white wine vinegar	500 mL
3 or 4	sprigs mixed herbs	3 or 4

☐ Wash the herbs and dry them between clean towels. Pack the herbs well into a 2 cup (500 mL) measuring cup and bruise them with a wooden spoon.

Meanwhile, bring the vinegar just to the simmering point. Immediately pour it over the herbs. Lay a plate over the measuring cup and let steep 24 hours.

Put 3 or 4 fresh sprigs of the same herbs in a sterilized bottle. Strain the vinegar, pressing the herbs well to extract all the color and flavoring juices. Pour through a coffee filter and then into the sterilized bottle. Cap with a plastic cork.

Suggested combinations for vinegar infusions:

■ Dill and garlic in white wine vinegar for fish dishes and cucumber salads.

■ Lemon balm, lemon thyme, a twist of lemon peel, and 5 or 6 peppercorns in white wine vinegar for marinades and grills of fish, chicken, or lamb.

■ Rosemary and thyme in red wine vinegar for grilled lamb or cold meat salads.

■ Sage, thyme, and a bay leaf in red wine vinegar as a seasoning for game birds.

About Dried Herbs and Spices

Much as we would all love to have fresh herbs billowing from little pots on every windowsill, the reality is usually something else. Dried herbs are the reasonable alternative, and with the exception of dried parsley, which is universally awful, they add greatly to the pleasure of cooking.

Although I usually prefer to blend herbs and spices myself, intriguing new blends are always coming onto the market. One that I do buy and use extensively is Jamaican jerk seasoning, a sweet spicy blend that was designed for meat but also enhances many vegetables.

Every cook needs a variety of single herbs and spices, purchased in small amounts because the flavor will have a relatively short shelf life. Store in a cool, dark spot, and if you haven't used your dried tarragon (basil, thyme, oregano, whatever) since last Christmas, be ruthless and pitch it out.

Other Essentials

Beyond oils and vinegars, herbs and spices, a few other flavoring agents and condiments are important to have on hand. A small investment buys a basic stock of each, and when inspiration or an emergency hits, you're already in the game.

- Fresh garlic and ginger root
- Lemons and limes
- Sun-dried tomatoes, either dry-pack or in oil (dry-pack is cheaper)
- Seasoned tomato sauce
- Chunky salsa, medium-hot or hot
- A good brand of tomato catsup
- Vine leaves in brine
- Roasted peppers in oil
- Small cans of sliced jalapenos
- Dry mustard, Dijon-style mustard, and a grainy, deli-style mustard
- Hot pepper sauce, Worcestershire sauce, soy sauce, thick teriyaki sauce
- A couple of jars of chutney, jalapeno jelly, a jar of pesto, and a decent antipasto relish are inspired additions to any kitchen. They'll serve you well in the inevitable pinch.

Part 2: Vegetable Recipes

A Few Words Before You Start

Some of the recipes in this book call for roasting hot peppers, peeling tomatoes and small onions, cooking dry beans, and making croutons. See the following for instructions or where to find additional information in the book.

■ **To roast hot peppers**, prick the peppers several times with a fork to keep them from bursting during roasting. Lay on a hot cast iron griddle and turn several times during roasting, allowing the skins to blister and char slightly. Pick them up with tongs, drop into a brown paper bag, and close the bag tightly for about 20 minutes. The peppers will steam as they cool, and you can peel the skins off under cold running water. Slit the peppers along the side, wash out the seeds, and pull out the core. Now they're ready to mince. Caution: Do not rub your eyes or touch your lips while handling chilies. Wash hands thoroughly afterward. The oils can cause painful burns.

■ **To peel tomatoes**, cover with boiling water for about 20 seconds, then plunge into cold water. The skins will slip off easily.

■ **To peel pearl or baby onions**, slice top and bottom off each little onion, pour boiling water over them, and leave for about 5 minutes. They'll peel easily, and you won't have to shed further tears.

■ **To quick soak dry beans** see section on Beans.

■ **To make croutons** see instructions in the following recipes: *Minestrone*, *Mesclun Salad*, *Not Exactly Caesar Salad*, and *Spinach Salad*.

Chapter 1 ■ Artichoke

ONE WAY OR ANOTHER, CIVILIZED PEOPLE HAVE BEEN EATING ARTICHOKES for about 2500 years. Yet in spite of artichokes' impressive lineage, many people still view them as expensive thistles, and their appearance at the table is generally greeted with public delight and private musings on boiling the cook in his or her own artichoke pot.

"Oooh, Rob, you've done artichokes! *Formidable!*" And then in a discrete whisper: "Mabel, I *told* you we should have gone bowling!"

It was ever thus. Around the second century A.D., Pliny the Elder, who had a lot to say about almost everything, hated artichokes. On a day when Mrs. Pliny evidently desired to serve them anyway, he worked himself into a snit over the event and made à cranky speech.

> *"See how vain and prodigal we be, to serve at our table these thistles which the very asses and other four-footed beasts have wit enough to avoid and refuse for fear of pricking their muzzles,"* he fumed.

But nobody listened to Pliny's whining, and artichokes continued to be eaten with great relish throughout the Aegean Islands, the western Mediterranean basin, and what we know today as the Middle East.

It was that tireless little gastronome, Catherine de Medici, who introduced them to the French when she married King Henry II (at age 15, if you please), after which they became known as a potent aphrodisiac. Suddenly, every Frenchman wanted some.

Their North American debut came around 1920 when they first appeared in California. They were planted by some enterprising Italian farmers near Castroville, where the climate was mild enough to keep the tender bracts from hardening and bursting into large purple flowers before they could put on the required flesh. Today, the Salinas Valley produces about 85 percent of the artichokes in North America.

Artichokes with Carrots and Potatoes, Greek Style

Artichokes in Pesto Cream with Tomatoes and Olives

IN THE MARKET: There are several varieties of artichoke, from the entirely edible, purplish buds so tender they can be eaten raw, to huge, lilac-tinted globes with exquisitely scalloped edges. Such exotic beauties seldom show up in North American markets, being products of those lucky gardens in the most salubrious regions of France and Italy. At the other extreme are magnificent near-thistles that grow wild in parts of the American southwest and end up in dried harvest arrangements of florists.

In most parts of North America, we eat the happy medium – firm, compact globes, a healthy green in spring with occasional light bronzing of the tips in November. This indicates a touch of frost, which doesn't hurt the choke. In fact, they'll likely be meatier and taste nuttier than the spring crop. Don't confuse the frost-kissed bronzing with the dry, withered browning of an artichoke that is simply old. If the leaves have begun to unfold like a flower trying to blossom, the globe is past its prime.

■ *Nutrition:* Eating artichokes by planting the leaf firmly between your front teeth and striping off the fleshy part is labor intensive, but it's nutritious. High in minerals (potassium and phosphorus) and vitamins C and A, the artichoke is low in calories.

■ *Season:* Prime is from March through May, with another less prolific season beginning in November.

■ *Buy:* 1 large artichoke per person.

IN THE KITCHEN: Store artichokes in the refrigerator in a perforated plastic bag, but do not wash before refrigerating. They'll hold for about a week.

When you're ready to cook them, slice off the top third of the leaves. This seems like a waste, but much of the globe is inedible, so be brutal. Pull off and discard the tough outer leaves, bending them back over your finger until they snap, and using kitchen scissors, snip off the sharp, thorny end of the remaining leaves. Most cookbooks advise whacking off the stem, but if you find artichokes with stems, leave them. Once peeled, they are a succulent part of the artichoke.

Immediately rub all cut surfaces with half a lemon to keep the flesh from darkening, or drop the artichoke into a bowl of acidulated water: 3 tbsp (45 mL) vinegar to 4 cups (1 L) of water.

To cook artichokes, drop into a large pot of boiling water to which you've added 1/4 cup (50 mL) each lemon juice and oil, plus 1 small, dried chili pepper. Simmer for as long as 40 minutes, depending upon the season and the size of the globe (small ones take less). Test by piercing the stem end with a paring knife. When tender, and when a leaf will pull away easily, the artichoke is done.

Drain artichokes upside down, squeezing gently between your palms to remove as much water as possible. Scoop out the fuzzy *choke* with a spoon and serve with hollandaise, melted butter, or a dipping sauce of your choice spooned into the middle. When you've almost run out of leaf-dippers and sauce, cut up the bottom and eat that, too.

Artichokes can also be stuffed, but I've always felt that life was too short.

Artichokes with Carrots and Potatoes, Greek Style

Another way to prepare artichokes is as my friend Janos does in the spring – Constantinople style with young potatoes and carrots, and the first fresh dill of the season. This dish is excellent for Easter with roast lamb or as a side dish with any grilled meat. I even like it solo, at room temperature, when the lemon and dill have had their way with the artichoke, leaving it tender and succulent, especially the stem, which develops a mellow, nutty flavor.

You will need the largest artichokes you can find for this because they have a fleshier bottom, which is what gives this dish its character.

Serves 6

6	large globe artichokes	6
6	young carrots	6
6	new potatoes	6
6	green onions or baby leeks	6
1	chicken bouillon cube	1
1/2 cup	olive oil	125 mL
	juice of 2 lemons	
1 tbsp	chopped dillweed	15 mL
1 tbsp	cornstarch	15 mL
1 1/2 cups	cooking liquid	375 mL
	salt and pepper	
	dillweed and lemon slices for garnish	

☐ Prepare artichokes for cooking. Parboil 30 minutes or longer, as directed above.

Drain, halve, remove all outside leaves, and scrape out the fuzzy choke, paring down to the few inner heart leaves and the bottom, leaving about 1 inch (2.5 cm) of stem.

Meanwhile, scrub but do not peel potatoes and carrots. Trim onions or leeks, leaving about an inch (2.5 cm) of green.

Now put artichokes, carrots, potatoes, and onions or baby leeks in a pan and add water to just cover. Bring to a simmer, stir in the chicken bouillon cube, crushed, and a grinding of black pepper. Cover and continue cooking until all vegetables are tender.

Put the olive oil, lemon juice, dillweed, and cornstarch in a small, lidded jar and shake until well-blended. Drain vegetables, reserving 1 1/2 cups (375 mL) of the cooking liquid, and return liquid to the pan with the vegetables. Stir the lemon-dill-cornstarch mixture into the vegetables and reduce heat to a bare simmer. Cook until sauce has thickened slightly. Taste for seasoning and correct if needed. Serve the vegetables and sauce in a shallow bowl, garnished with dill fronds and thin slices of lemon.

Artichokes in Pesto Cream with Tomatoes and Olives

This is a wonderful recipe for lazy cooks. Because it uses marinated artichokes, most of the work is already done for you. Marinated artichokes can be found at Italian or Greek markets, where you can buy them in large, economical jars. The 24 oz (750 mL) jar packed by Unico yields just over 2 cups (500 mL) of artichoke hearts and a bit less than a cup (250 mL) of delicious, oily vinaigrette, a bonus for a later salad.

If you're making this in the winter or are using commercial pesto, taste it to be sure it has enough basil and be prepared to add a few extra leaves, finely minced. Fresh basil has incredible aroma and flavor, and adds a sweet, delicately spicy note to this simple dish. Serve with a hearth bread such as focaccia (see recipe for focaccia in section on Herbs).

Serves 6

2 cups	marinated artichoke hearts	500 mL
1/2 cup	black olives, pitted	125 mL
1 cup	cherry tomatoes, halved	250 mL
1/2 cup	whipped salad dressing	125 mL
1/4 cup	basil pesto	50 mL
1/3 cup	freshly grated Parmesan cheese	75 mL
	freshly grated black pepper	
	additional fresh parsley and basil, if needed	

☐ Drain the artichokes, reserving the marinade for later use.

Place artichokes in a large, glass bowl with the olives and cherry tomatoes. If the artichokes are very large, slice lengthwise into smaller, bite-size pieces.

The Decorative Artichoke:

Hollowed out artichokes make lovely candle holders for a low table setting. Buy large ones, trim the stem end evenly so the artichoke will sit upright, and scoop out the middle with a spoon so you can fit a glass votive candle holder in it.

Dry the artichokes for several days, then spray with gold paint. Place the votive candles in them and set among low arrangements of seasonal greenery and vegetables. At Christmas, they look especially festive set among live evergreens with sprigs of red berries.

Whisk together the whipped salad dressing, the pesto, and the Parmesan. Pour over the vegetables and fold everything together, adding a hefty grinding of black pepper. Taste the mixture, adding salt as needed. Keeps well, refrigerated, for two or three days.

Seashell Pasta Variation: Increase the amount of pesto by 2 tbsp (30 mL) and fold in 2 cups (500 mL) of cooked conchigliette (small seashell pasta) or rotini.

Chapter 2 ▪ Asparagus

IF WINTER COMES, CAN ASPARAGUS BE FAR BEHIND? WITH APOLOGIES to Percy Bysshe Shelley, it's not a skylark, but the first local asparagus that is the true harbinger of spring.

Now that asparagus is available from Mexico almost year-round, some of the anticipation of the first tender stalks has gone, but I still wait impatiently to catch local asparagus and enjoy it more than ever.

IN THE MARKET: Look for asparagus that is bright green with moist stem ends (ideally, these should be resting in water or damp florist's moss) and tight, closed tips. Unless you're at a farmers market where you know the local crop has just been harvested, be sure the vendor has them well misted. Regardless of the thickness of the stem – some like it thin, others want a fat spear – asparagus must always be crisp. If the spear flops over when you pick it up, put it back and revise your menu.

▪ *Nutrition:* Rich in vitamin A, fair amount of vitamin C, and contains some iron. Low in calories – about 40 calories per cup (250 mL), chopped and cooked.

▪ *Season:* From early March through June the asparagus crop is at its peak, with fresh local asparagus always your first choice. Mexican asparagus is now available almost year-round.

▪ *Buy:* If you're serious about asparagus, buy six spears per person. I like a whole meal of it with nothing but asparagus and a sauce to dip it in, and if you're going that route, you'll need a few more spears.

IN THE KITCHEN: Soak a paper towel with water and wrap the cut ends the instant you get the asparagus home. Slip the entire bunch into a plastic bag and refrigerate. Properly sealed, it will keep three or four days in the refrigerator.

Asparagus with Balsamic Vinegar

Grilled Asparagus with Herb Cream

Asparagus Picnic Rolls

To prepare for cooking, snap the stem end off where it breaks naturally, reserving that bit for stock. Peel the stem if necessary. Wash the tops *gently* in cold water to remove sand and grit.

I like to steam asparagus by standing the spears upright in my old aluminum coffee pot for about 10 minutes, depending on the thickness of the stems. When they're easily pierced with a paring knife, they're done.

Asparagus can also be boiled, microwaved, or stir-fried. Remember that the thicker stems will hold the heat and continue to cook a little more, even after you've taken them out of the steam. Whatever method you choose, you can't go wrong with asparagus, as long as you don't overcook it.

 *from The Garden*

Asparagus with Balsamic Vinegar

Marinated asparagus is an outstanding spring hors d'oeuvre, served cool or at room temperature. Use either balsamic or black rice vinegar in the marinade. Although their flavors are distinctly different, both have a dark, mellow flavor that enhances the fresh green taste of asparagus.

Trim the bottom of the stalks so guests aren't wandering around with long drippy pieces of asparagus in hand – this is finger food. It also makes a good salad for the buffet table, especially at brunch with any egg or cheese dish. If you have a choice, fat stalky spears work better in this dish than the longer, slender ones.

Serves 4 to 6

24	spears asparagus	24
1/2 cup	flavorful olive oil	125 mL
3 tbsp	balsamic or black rice vinegar	45 mL
	salt and freshly ground pepper	

☐ Steam asparagus spears until just tender. Meanwhile, prepare marinade by shaking together the oil, vinegar, salt, and pepper.

Drain asparagus. Lay the spears in a glass dish and while still a little warm, pour the marinade over them. Turn several times during the next hour or two, and serve at room temperature.

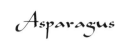

Grilled Asparagus with Herb Cream

Grilled asparagus is a luxurious first course, yet few people bother with it. If the stalks are fat, steam them a little first to ensure even cooking, then finish them on the barbecue. This will impart a smoky, slightly charred sweetness to the vegetable.

Offer grilled asparagus with a cool, silky yogurt sauce, full of the flavors and scents of new green herbs, which must be fresh for this particular dish. Use a few leaves of lovage, a few leaves of parsley, a wisp of tarragon or cilantro (not both), and some chives.

Serves 4 to 6

24	thick spears asparagus	24
	olive oil	

Yogurt Sauce

1 cup	skim milk yogurt	250 mL
1/2 cup	light sour cream	125 mL
1/4 cup	creamy cucumber dressing	50 mL
	or	
1/4 cup	mayonnaise	50 mL
1/2 cup	finely minced spring herbs	125 mL
	salt and white pepper to taste	

☐ Make the sauce by whisking together yogurt, sour cream, creamy cucumber dressing, minced herbs, and salt and pepper.

Steam asparagus just until the color brightens – no more than 5 minutes. At this point, the asparagus may be covered and refrigerated until you have the barbecue fired up.

To cook, brush asparagus spears with olive oil. Lay them on an oiled grill over hot coals. Cook about 5 minutes, turning several times as the skin begins to bronze and char slightly. Serve on small plates with a spoonful of the sauce and some grilled ripe tomatoes.

Asparagus Picnic Rolls

The best picnics are spontaneous events brought on by a sudden day of leisure time and splendiferous weather. It's best to just throw something into a basket and go, before the urge to escape leaves you or the rain starts. This is just such a dish.

The asparagus, lightly cooked but still somewhat crisp, is bundled in a blanket of ham, cheese, and yeast dough, then baked. Some Sunday morning in summer when you need an easy picnic, you'll be glad you know about this recipe. Or try it on a magic June night down by the river. Either way, it's one of those shameless shortcuts that make life easier.

For convenience, I've suggested using refrigerated dough, the large croissants that come in a tube and need only be unrolled. Thawed, frozen bread dough can also be used if you're the plan-ahead type, and if you have the time or inclination to make your own dough, it will probably be even better.

Serves 4

1	large pkg refrigerated croissant dough	1
12	asparagus spears, steamed and cooled	12
4	thin slices black forest ham	4
1 cup	sharp Cheddar, grated	250 mL
1	egg	1
1 tbsp	water	15 mL
	extra Cheddar	

☐ Preheat oven to 400 F (200 C).

Unroll croissant dough and separate into four triangles.

On each triangle, lay a thin slice of ham, trimmed if necessary (it need not be a perfect fit), and sprinkle each with 1/4 cup (50 mL) grated Cheddar. Lay 3 lightly steamed asparagus spears on each triangle and roll the dough up, starting from the wide end. Make egg wash by beating one egg with 1 tbsp (15 mL) cold water. Brush rolls with egg wash and sprinkle with additional Cheddar. Bake until golden brown. If packing for a picnic, wrap the rolls in a napkin after cooling briefly.

If the heat of the day is over and your picnic spot offers access to a grill, wrap the cooled rolls with aluminum foil so they can be re-heated. This makes a terrific picnic supper, along with a cool bottle of white wine.

Chapter 3 ▪ Avocado

AVOCADOS ALWAYS MAKE ME THINK OF TUESDAYS.

When I was a newcomer to the newsroom, Tuesday was a day of considerable stress. It was the day my food and wine section was put together, and anything that could go wrong usually did. I'd hold up pretty well until about 5 p.m., by which time the stacks of paper on my desk were defying gravity, essential photographs had been mislaid, my left eye started twitching, and I'd forget how to spell tough words like *spoon* and *egg*.

Around 7 p.m., an understanding friend would lead me out of the building and into a restaurant, where I longed to dive into a large martini pitcher. One night, seeking solace in a bowl of guacamole, I discovered IT – the joy of avocados.

Avocados are so gently, sensuously rounded outside and so meltingly cream-cheese soft inside that they're extremely soothing to body and soul. And they're so packed with all the right nutrients that they've become one of nature's great tranquilizers.

IN THE MARKET: There are dozens of varieties of avocado with wonderful names like Lula, Choquette, and Zutano. One of my favorites is Fuerte, the Spanish word for strong, so named because it survived the great California freeze of 1913, which wiped out its more delicate relatives. Eighty-five percent of our avocados come from California, and they tend to be smaller, higher in fat, and more full flavored than their larger Florida cousins.

Avocados are born green and they stay green, with some of them shading to near black. Fuerte is a bright green, smooth-skinned fruit with a classic pear shape and a mild flavor. Hass is a larger, oval-shaped pear with bumpy skin that turns from dark green to nearly black as it matures. It's an excellent avocado, with rich, buttery flesh and a nutlike flavor. Zutano is smaller than Hass, with smooth skin, a higher ratio of pit to flesh, and a milder flavor. The texture is not as buttery as Hass.

Avocado BLT

Guacamole with Cilantro, Xtapa Style

Avocado, Tomato and Grapefruit Ribbons with Honey Lime Dressing

Avocado Sunburst with Oranges and Peppered Strawberries

from The Garden

Most markets stock avocados underripe, when the flesh is hard. To check ripeness, hold the avocado in your palm and press gently – when ripe, it will yield. Buy softer avocados to eat today, hard ones to keep for two days or so.

Avoid avocados that have soft spots, visible bruises, or a missing stem-button.

■ **Nutrition:** A single avocado contains from 150 to 180 calories per half. Though high in fat (up to 30 percent of its flesh weight may be oil), it's 70 percent monounsaturated. Avocados provide 14 vitamins, including A, several of the B vitamins, plus C and E, and small amounts of 11 minerals.

■ **Season:** Avocados are available from somewhere, in some variety, year-round. Fuerte is most abundant during the winter months. Hass comes into the markets in the spring and is with us until late autumn, just in time for the return of the formidable little Fuerte.

■ **Buy:** Count on 1/2 avocado per person.

IN THE KITCHEN: Refrigerate until ready for ripening. It will hold nicely for about a week. To ripen, place avocados in a brown paper bag at room temperature. They emit natural ethylene gas, the same gas used to turn green tomatoes a pretty shade of red.

To store half an avocado, leave the pit in, brush the cut surface with lemon juice, wrap tightly with plastic, and refrigerate.

There are numerous recipes for cooked avocado, but you won't find them here. Much as I love the buttery, golden-green flesh of a perfectly ripened avocado, I wouldn't give a nickel for a truckload of cooked avocado. The flavor either dissipates or grows bitter, and the color develops a nasty gray tinge.

Fast-Track Avocados

■ Slice a ripe avocado over an omelet. Top with sour cream and salsa.

■ Mash a ripe avocado and spread it on toasted English muffin halves. Top with mozzarella, sweet red onion, and a squeeze of lime juice. Broil just long enough to melt the cheese – the onion should still be crunchy.

■ Mash 2 avocados with the juice of a lime and stir in prepared salsa to taste. Instant guacamole!

■ Fill avocado halves with curried shrimp salad.

■ Fold together diced avocado, any cooked seafood, freshly chopped dill, and a good mayonnaise. Serve on pumpernickel as an open-face sandwich.

Avocado BLT

This upscaled version of the classic blt makes a wonderful supper for a lazy night with something good on television. The ripe avocado replaces the butter in a fresh, crusty baguette, and what a butter it is – golden-green, soft, smooth, nutty. There's nothing wrong with using leaf lettuce here, but I prefer reliable old iceberg for its magnificent crunch.

Serves 2

1	baguette, sliced lengthwise	1
1	large avocado, mashed	1
1 tsp	lemon or lime juice	5 mL
	salt and pepper	
1	large tomato, sliced	1
4	slices bacon, cooked crisp	4
	iceberg lettuce, shredded	
	sweet red onion, thinly sliced	
	mayonnaise	

☐ To assemble the BLT, mash the avocado coarsely with lemon or lime juice, salt, and pepper. Generously spread the bottom half of the baguette with it. Top the avocado with tomato slices, cooked bacon slices, shredded iceberg lettuce, and a few thin slices of sweet red onion. Spread the top half of the baguette with mayonnaise. Voilà, a great sandwich!

 *from The Garden*

Guacamole with Cilantro, Xtapa Style

There's a lot of guacamole around – some of it is made with cream cheese, garlic powder, even ketchup. Such down-and-dirty cookin' does the avocado no favors. If you love avocados, try this gutsy version of the classic, mashed avocado sauce.

Instead of thumping everything into a blender for a too-smooth finish, this guacamole is made the traditional way by mashing the avocado with a fork, or even a mortar and pestle if you want to be authentic. It's a textured guacamole in which your teeth will continually encounter little nuggets of crisp sweet onion and ripe tomato. The buttery flesh of the avocado complements them perfectly, and when you add the sharp, clear flavors of garlic and fresh lime juice, the warmth of roasted chilies, and the refreshing bite of cilantro, this simple sauce becomes an event. Serve it in a bright pottery bowl with blue corn chips and sliced jicama. Bring on the beer. A pitcher of margaritas wouldn't hurt either.

This is a lovely winter dish, especially with Hass avocados. Be sure they're ripe before you start.

Serves 4 to 6

2	large ripe avocados	2
	juice of 1 large lime	
1 tsp	salt	5 mL
2	jalapeno peppers, roasted	2
1	tomato, diced	1
1/2 cup	red onion, minced	125 mL
2	cloves garlic, pressed	2
1/2 tsp	cumin	2 mL
2 tbsp	chopped cilantro	30 mL
	salt to taste	

☐ Peel and pit avocados. Mash them coarsely with the juice of one lime and the salt. Finely mince roasted jalapenos. Stir in the jalapenos, tomato, onion, garlic, cumin, and cilantro. (If using canned jalapenos, the flavor will change slightly, but don't worry, it will still be delicious.) Taste the guacamole for salt and correct the seasoning if necessary.

Tomatillo Variation: This is a good sauce to serve with enchiladas or scrambled eggs. Just simmer half a dozen fresh husked tomatillos in a little water for about 10 minutes. Drain. As soon as you can handle them, mince and stir into the guacamole.

Tomato Variation: Omit red onion. Add 2 large, firm tomatoes, peeled and diced, and 2 green onions, minced. Correct the salt, as it will need a touch more because of the acid in the tomatoes.

Avocado, Tomato and Grapefruit Ribbons with Honey Lime Dressing

Avocados and tomatoes are one of the great food marriages, a near-perfect balance of gentle and assertive, mellow and sharp. In this dish, use a firm tomato, but be sure it's fully ripe.

Arranged in ribbons on an oval or rectangular platter, this salad looks smashing as part of a cold buffet with baked ham and some interesting bread, or with a casserole of baked enchiladas.

Serves 6

2	large avocados	2
2	large tomatoes	2
2	large pink grapefruit	2
1 cup	sliced black olives	250 mL

Honey Lime Dressing

1/2 cup	low-fat yogurt	125 mL
1/4 cup	canola oil	50 mL
1/4 cup	liquid honey	50 mL
1 tsp	grated lime rind	5 mL
1/2 cup	lime juice	125 mL
1/4 cup	fresh parsley, minced	50 mL
1/2 tsp	salt	2 mL

☐ Place ingredients for the dressing in a jar and shake until emulsified.

Peel and dice avocado and place in a small glass bowl. Immediately pour a little of the dressing over it and toss gently to coat. This will prevent the avocado from turning brown.

Peel and dice tomatoes.

Peel grapefruit, pull it into sections, and carefully strip as much of the membrane away as possible. Arrange grapefruit sections diagonally across an oval or rectangular platter. Line both sides of the grapefruit with a thin ribbon of sliced black olives. Distribute the tomato and avocado in alternating ribbons on either side of the grapefruit. Drizzle with additional dressing.

For a larger party, double the recipe and arrange in a stylized S pattern across the platter, like ribbons floating in the wind.

Avocado Sunburst with Oranges and Peppered Strawberries

Pepper, balsamic vinegar, and strawberries are a flavor combination I first tasted in a kitchen in Italy when the berries were slightly underripe, and I was amazed at the results. Under no circumstances should you use pre-ground pepper. This dish requires the flavor, aroma, and bite of coarse, freshly ground pepper berries.

Serves 6 to 8

4	large navel oranges	4
3 cups	fresh strawberries	750 mL
2 tbsp	balsamic vinegar	30 mL
1 tsp	granulated sugar	5 mL
	coarsely ground black pepper	
2	avocados	2
	juice of 1 lemon or lime	

Strawberry Lime Vinaigrette

1 cup	strawberries, crushed	250 mL
1/2 tsp	grated lime rind	2 mL
	juice of 1 lime	
1 tbsp	balsamic vinegar	15 mL
1 tsp	honey	5 mL

Put vinaigrette ingredients in a blender and liquefy.

Peel oranges and separate into segments. With a small, sharp knife, carefully remove as much membrane as possible.

☐ Hull most of the strawberries, reserving a few with the brightest stem caps as garnish. Place berries in a glass bowl. Sprinkle with balsamic vinegar, sugar, and a generous grinding of coarse black pepper. Turn berries gently, just to acquaint them with the vinegar.

Peel the avocados and slice lengthwise, turning immediately in lemon or lime juice to prevent discoloration.

On a large round serving platter, alternate avocado and orange sections in a sunburst pattern, leaving a space in the center. Pile the strawberries in the middle, placing those with green hulls around the top.

Drizzle a ribbon of the bright red vinaigrette over top.

Chapter 4 ■ Beans

Grandma used to save her most scathing condemnations for people who were bone-lazy and "wouldn't amount to a hilla beans." I understood about bone-lazy, but she lost me on the beans. Ever since I was a kid I've had beans in my garden, and they've been anything but lazy. In fact, a hill of beans is frequently so prolific that there are beans climbing the fence, beans lopping over onto the sidewalk, beans to freeze, to pickle, to share with the neighbors.

Picking beans is not an unpleasant chore. In itself, it's a peaceful pursuit, beginning with the small thrill of discovery when you lift the leaves and there they hang – slender, graceful, drooping.

The history of the humble bean reaches as far back as biblical times. Lentils were especially favored among the ancients: Greeks, Romans, Hebrews, and Egyptians. Talk about your staying power – it is believed that the dried beans we rely on today are of the same type that were cultivated 8000 years ago by Peruvian Indians.

IN THE MARKET: Unhappily, fresh beans in the supermarket suffer from having been picked days before. All their natural, tender sweetness has flown, and they're often too old and leathery to be bothered with. Especially useless are the Chinese longbeans, which seem always to arrive at the market withered and spotty.

The best thing, of course, is to grow your own. Even in a cool climate, it's possible to have a bean garden as they take little space and grow well in any sunny spot. No garden? Farmers markets and you-picks are always a good bet. Look for a crisp, bright, slender pod free of bruises or brown spots.

Now, for the purpose of sounding organized, let me divide beans into three general categories.

■ *Snap Beans:* These are long, slender beans, which once had a tough string along their entire length and were therefore known as string beans. Other people know them as bush beans or pole beans, depending on their particular growing habits.

Since plant breeders have eliminated the strings, we enjoy, with considerably less effort, a wide range of these delicious beans in colors ranging from the green Blue Lake type (look for Provider or Jade, as well as the flat, broad Italian Romanos) to yellow wax beans to purple beans that turn green when cooked.

■ **Shell Beans:** A second category includes baby limas, small, jet-black soybeans, the flat, green soybeans called butterbeans, and the broad, meaty fava bean, as well as the French favorite, the flageolet. This hard-to-find bean has a long, slender pod holding 8 to 10 tiny, bright green beans.

Many markets now offer shell beans fresh during their short season, and they're meltingly delicious when steamed with a little butter.

■ **Dried Beans:** When the season ends, shell beans spill into a third category for which you can turn to any good market, especially the ethnic markets.

Dried beans, which began as fresh shell beans, include tiny, dark red adzuki, little black turtle beans, the larger coffee-and-cream colored pinto beans, several varieties of meaty Italian cannelini, the lovely pink-and-white cranberry beans, the reliable little Great Northerns, and the slightly smaller navy beans, plus red or green lentils, which aren't, strictly speaking, the same thing as beans.

So cheap, filling, nutritious, and all-around useful is the bean that it's a true international. I've eaten wonderful bean dishes in Italy, France, Spain, and the Netherlands, and they have told me more about the cooks and their particular circumstances than a dozen textbooks could have.

■ **Nutrition:** Excellent source of fiber, vegetable protein, iron, and complex carbohydrates. Good source of vitamins A and B, riboflavin, thiamin, and niacin, with some calcium and phosphorus.

By combining legumes, which includes not just beans but peas and lentils, with nuts, seeds, or milk products such as cheese, we balance the essential amino acids for a complete protein, a fact that is of special importance to vegetarians.

■ **Season:** May through August for edible pod beans.

■ **Buy:** 4 to 6 oz (115 to 170 grams) of fresh beans per person. One cup (250 mL) of dried beans will yield 3 cups (750 mL) of soaked, cooked beans.

IN THE KITCHEN: *Snap Beans:* Green or yellow snap beans can be kept in the refrigerator, in plastic, for three to four days.

Once, when Ed and I were staying in a house in Italy, the cook, Lillianna, had a bumper crop of green beans in her garden. She would braise them with tomatoes and butter, or stir-fry them with garlic, but she never brought them to the table without first running out to the patio with a bean impaled on a fork, looking for somebody to sample them, checking for readiness. You'll find that cooking time will vary with the variety of bean, the size, and the way they're cut, and the way to know when they're done is Lillianna's way – bite into it.

Dried Beans: If you haven't time to sort, soak, and bake, much can be done with a good brand of canned beans. Unlike most vegetables, shell beans take extremely well to canning. Two Italian companies, Unico and Primo, offer a wide variety of unflavored canned beans, as does the Dutch company, Honig. These products work well in casseroles and soups, and save time and effort right off the bat. Frozen beans are also a good option if you treat them well. With beans, as with so many vegetables, the cook's intuition and common sense are the most important ingredients.

Quick soak method: Bring water to a boil in a large pot, using 3 cups (750 mL) unsalted water to 1 cup (250 mL) beans. Add dried beans, return to a boil, and cook gently for 2 minutes. Don't let it come to a rolling boil as it may split some of the beans and toughen their skins.

Turn off the heat and let beans sit approximately 1 hour, covered. The steeping time will vary depending on the type of bean, with small lima beans taking about 45 minutes, large lima, navy, and pinto beans taking an hour or more, and kidney and cranberry beans taking closer to 2 hours. Check for tenderness – the texture should be chewy, even crisp, but no longer rock-hard and brittle. Drain, rinse, and proceed with your recipe. At this point, they're ready to use in any recipe as you would fresh, shelled beans.

The Only Bean Casserole

The reason for the name is that even if you never learn to cook another dish from scratch, this one will keep you and your friends healthy and sassy forever.

More method than recipe, it costs less, feeds more people, and is generally more useful and adaptable than any other single dish I can think of.

Strictly speaking, it's not just a bean dish, but a bean and grain dish. You'll need a cup (250 mL) of mixed things – dried beans, barley, lentils, split peas, wild or brown rice. The more variety, the better. In this dish, don't worry about lumping different beans into the same soaking time. The beans and lentils will be tender and mealy, the split peas firm, the wild rice chewy, the barley pillowy, and the whole thing will be lightened by the vegetables and strengthened by the meat. And it will expand enormously due to a miracle ingredient – water.

The Only contains very little meat, and while ham sausage is mentioned here because I have a source of terrific double-smoked, you can use virtually any meat – leftover, fresh, or smoked; turkey, ham, ground beef, or pork – check the refrigerator and call the neighbors.

The Only will feed eight the first day, or you can serve two and turn the leftovers into a great pot of minestrone to feed a crowd the second day.

Day One – The Casserole

1 cup	mixed dried beans and grains	250 mL
3 cups	cold water	750 mL
1	onion	1
1	green pepper	1
1	carrot	1
2	cloves garlic, pressed	2
1 cup	sliced ham sausage	250 mL
1/4 cup ea	ketchup and molasses	50 mL ea
1 cup	seasoned tomato sauce	250 mL
1 tsp	cinnamon	5 mL
1 tbsp	chili powder	15 mL
	or	
1 tbsp	Jamaican jerk seasoning	15 mL
3 cups	water	750 mL
	salt and pepper	

☐ Place beans and grains in a pot with 3 cups (750 mL) cold water. Bring to a gentle boil for 2 minutes. Turn off heat, cover pot, and let mixture steep for 1 hour.

Meanwhile, dice onion, pepper, and carrot.

When quick soak is complete, drain and rinse beans. Pour into a bean pot or 12 cup (3 L) casserole. Stir into the pot the diced vegetables, garlic, ham sausage, ketchup, molasses, tomato sauce, cinnamon, and chili powder. (Add salt later, as it toughens legumes.)

Stir in 3 cups (750 mL) water, adding more as needed during baking.

Cover the pot and bake at 300 F (150 C) for about 3 hours, checking to make sure the beans don't dry out, adding more water as necessary.

When beans are cooked but still firm, add salt and pepper to taste. Serve with raw vegetables, fresh bread, and grated Cheddar cheese for sprinkling over the beans.

Sloppy Josephina Variation: For each serving, cut the top third off a large crusty dinner roll and hollow the bottom out, leaving an inch (2.5 cm) of shell and reserving the tops. Brush the inside with soft butter, and bake in a 350 F (180 C) oven until lightly toasted. Reserve until time to serve. These can be done a day ahead.

Warm the hollowed rolls in the oven. For each serving, place a roll in a pasta dish or cream soup plate and fill generously with The Only, letting a little run over. Prop the lid beside it. Serve with raw vegetables – radishes, green onions, and sweet peppers.

Day Two – The Minestrone

Now comes the bonus. If you've only used two or three servings of The Only, you'll have almost 5 cups (1 L to 1.25 L) left to prop up your wonderful minestrone.

Do not confuse this with the watery vegetable brew that passes for minestrone in some restaurants. What you have here is a hefty winter soup to simmer slowly, thoughtfully, for a melding of flavors and textures. No single vegetable should stand out. Rather, this pot will hold a harmonious blend with the original beans adding authority, and additional broth and vegetables lending flavor.

Serves 10 to 12

4 to 5 cups	leftover *The Only*	1 to 1.25 L
1	small cabbage	1
1	28 oz (796 mL) can tomatoes in juice	1
3 cups	water	750 mL
1 tsp	oregano	5 mL
1 tsp	sugar	5 mL
1 tbsp	lemon juice	15 mL
1/2 cup	rice or orzo	125 mL
	salt and pepper to taste	

☐ Place leftover bean mixture in a large Dutch oven.

Shred cabbage and stir into The Only. Add the tomatoes, breaking them up with the back of a spoon.

Add water and bring the mixture to a simmer. Let it perk away on low heat for about 30 minutes.

Add oregano, sugar, lemon juice, rice or orzo (other pasta may be substituted), and cook another 20 minutes. Taste and correct the seasonings with salt and pepper, if necessary. Let the soup rest about 10 more minutes while the flavors ripen and you run some croutons into the oven, one per person.

To serve this soup, sprinkle the croutons with freshly grated Parmesan or Asiago cheese. Place a crouton in the bottom of each warmed soup bowl and ladle the minestrone over it.

Croutons

In this book, a crouton is not a cube of stale bread from a cardboard box, but a slice of good baguette, brushed liberally with a garlic-infused oil and baked until crisp. This takes about 15 minutes at 300 F (150 C), after which the oven can be turned off and the croutons left inside with the door ajar to further crisp them. Croutons can be stored in a jar for three or four days, but they're best fresh.

Lentil Soup with Balsamic Swirl

The ancient lentil is back again, and it's especially handy for the cook as it requires no pre-soaking. Lentils will double in size during cooking.

Lentil soup is one of the great wintery dishes, as comforting and sustaining as it is warming. This one is as thick as a stew and gets a surprising bash of flavor from the aromatic Jamaican jerk seasoning (found in ethnic markets and most supermarkets) and the balsamic sauce that is swirled into each bowl.

Serves 8

3 cups	dry red or green lentils	750 mL
8 cups	chicken stock	2 L
4	cloves garlic, pressed	4
1	large onion, diced	1
2	stalks celery with leaves, diced	2
1	large carrot, diced	1
1 tsp	oregano	5 mL
1/2 tsp	thyme	2 mL
1 tbsp	Jamaican jerk seasoning	15 mL
	salt and freshly ground pepper to taste	

Balsamic Sauce

1/4 cup	balsamic or red wine vinegar	50 mL
1/2 cup	plain yogurt	125 mL
1/4 cup	freshly minced parsley	50 mL
2 tbsp	freshly minced cilantro	30 mL

☐ In a large Dutch oven, bring lentils and chicken stock to a boil. Immediately reduce heat to simmer for 30 minutes.

Add remaining soup ingredients, and continue simmering for 30 minutes longer. Taste to correct salt. If soup is too thick to suit you, thin it with additional chicken stock or a little water.

Meanwhile, make the sauce. Put all ingredients in a jar and shake well.

As you serve each bowl of soup, put about 2 tbsp (30 mL) of the sauce in the middle and swirl it with a fork.

Two Great Chili Recipes

I can't write about beans without getting into chili, at least briefly. There are as many chilies as there are cooks, including all-meat, no-meat, seafood, chicken, rattlesnake, mild, medium, or screamin' hot. There are even, God knows why, no-bean chilies. Having judged a few chili contests and concocted tubs of the stuff for my own family, I've seldom met one I didn't like. From an astonishing array of possible chilies, I offer two. Both owe their strength of character to beans.

My chili recipes are all big, which is really the only way to make good chili. If you aren't serving a crowd, freeze the leftovers.

Three Bean Chili with Duck and Chocolate

Here's a dark, wintery chili, full of earthy flavors, a proper meal for a cold night or a weekend lunch when home is the skier, home from the hill...

Oddly enough, it's distantly related to a great dish from the southwest of France, *cassoulet*. It takes its character from the richness of the duck meat and sausage, but the addition of chocolate is a Mexican tradition that deepens the flavor.

Fresh shell beans will be impossible to find in winter. By all means, use dried beans from scratch if you have the time and inclination, but I use good quality canned beans, which makes this one of the easiest of all winter casseroles for a crowd.

No time to do a duck? A barbecued duck, or selected pieces thereof from a Chinese market, is an inspired replacement. ❯

Three Bean Chili with Duck and Chocolate

Serves 12

1	19 oz (540 mL) can garbanzo beans, drained	1
1	19 oz (540 mL) can black beans, drained	1
1	19 oz (540 mL) can baked beans with molasses	1
4 lb	duck, cut up	2 kg
1/4 cup	olive oil	50 mL
1	carrot, chopped	1
1	large onion, diced	1
1	stalk celery with leaves, chopped	1
4	cloves garlic, pressed	4
2 tbsp	chili powder	30 mL
1 tsp ea	cumin and cinnamon	5 mL ea
1/2 tsp	ground cloves	2 mL
4 tbsp	cocoa	60 mL
1 tbsp	dark molasses	15 mL
8 oz	smoked sausage, sliced	250 g
1 cup	dry red wine	250 mL
	green onion tops, minced	
	sour cream or yogurt	

☐ Layer beans in a Dutch oven.

In a large frying pan, brown duck parts in olive oil. Tuck duck into beans.

In the duck drippings, brown the carrot, onion, and celery. Add garlic, chili powder, cumin, cinnamon, and cloves. Stir in cocoa and molasses. Pour over duck and beans.

Scatter sliced sausage over the vegetable layer. Pour red wine over sausages. Cover and bake in a 350 F (180 C) oven for 1 hour, stirring after 30 minutes. If casserole appears to be drying out, add a splash more wine. Taste for seasoning, adding more chili powder if you wish.

Sprinkle with minced green onion tops, and serve with sour cream or yogurt on the side.

A salad of crisp greenery and a loaf of warm bread complete this meal, especially if you can produce a bottle of young, fruity Beaujolais or some cold beer to go with it.

Summer Chili with Shell Beans, Grilled Vegetables and Baby Corn

Summer chili comes straight from the garden with fresh vegetables and just enough meat to give it courage. For this chili, the chicken and most of the vegetables are first grilled, then added to the bean pot where they give it exceptional depth of flavor and a hint of smoke. Use fresh shell beans in season, but the dish is as good with canned or frozen beans if you decide to make summer chili in the winter.

The length of the ingredient list seems daunting, but just keep thumping them into the pot – it goes together quickly and is worth a bit of effort.

Serves 10 to 12

	olive oil	
2	chicken breasts, boned	2
1	large yellow bell pepper, quartered	1
1	medium Japanese eggplant, sliced diagonally	1
1	large onion, sliced inch-thick	1
3	cloves garlic, pressed	3
1	19 oz (540 mL) can baby corn cobs	1
1/4 cup	hot salsa	50 mL
1 tbsp	brown sugar	15 mL
2 tbsp	chili powder	30 mL
8	ripe tomatoes, peeled and quartered	8
2 cups	rich chicken stock	500 mL
2 cups	fresh or canned kidney beans	500 mL
2 cups	baby lima beans	500 mL
	freshly minced parsley, oregano, cilantro	
	salt to taste	

☐ Preheat broiler.

Brush chicken, yellow pepper, eggplant, and onion with oil. Place under the broiler, in two batches if necessary. Turn everything once, watching closely to make sure the chicken doesn't burn. Remove the vegetables as they brown and begin to char. Do not remove the charred bits.

Cut chicken in thick slices and lay in a large Dutch oven. Dice vegetables coarsely and add them to the pot along with the garlic, baby corn, salsa, brown sugar, chili powder, and tomatoes. Add chicken stock and beans, and simmer on a medium-hot burner for about 30 minutes. (If using canned kidney beans, drain; frozen limas need not be defrosted.) Stir in fresh herbs. Salt to taste. Add more chili powder and/or salsa if desired.

Serve with rice and sour cream, a loaf of sourdough bread, and cold beer.

Lima Beans with Tomato, Greek Style

You might as well make a potful of these while you're at it because it takes the same amount of time to soak a lot as a little and they freeze well. This dish is best served at room temperature, as part of an antipasto plate or a salad buffet. Frozen lima beans, cooked and drained, will work very well here, but dried lima beans will give it the best texture. The large, meaty beans have a satisfying chewiness for a winter meal. In summer, this is delicious made with fresh fava beans.

Serves 8

2 cups	dried large lima beans	500 mL
2 tbsp	olive oil	30 mL
2	large onions, peeled, sliced lengthwise	2
4	cloves garlic, pressed	4
1 tsp	thyme	5 mL
2 cups	thick tomato sauce	500 mL
1	small lemon, quartered, thinly sliced	1
1/2 tsp	cinnamon	2 mL
2 tsp	sugar	5 mL
	salt and pepper to taste	
	green onion, finely minced	

☐ In a Dutch oven, cover the dried lima beans with water. Bring to a boil for 2 minutes, then turn off heat. Let the beans soak for a bit more than an hour, or until no longer hard to the bite.

Meanwhile, heat oil in a large frying pan. Sauté onions, garlic, and thyme until onion is transparent, but don't brown. Add tomato sauce, lemon, cinnamon, and sugar.

Simmer the sauce about 5 minutes. Drain limas and add to sauce. Continue cooking another 20 minutes or so. The length of cooking time will depend on the quality and age of the beans. Beans should be tender but still firm enough to resist the teeth slightly. Taste for seasoning, adding a touch more cinnamon if you wish.

Refrigerate beans overnight to let the flavors ripen. Serve at room temperature with finely minced green onion strewn over top.

If you have leftovers and don't want to freeze them, stir into a casserole of regular baked beans or incorporate in a bean salad.

 *From The Garden*

Butter-Steamed Snap Beans

Summer vegetables don't get easier, or better, than fresh green beans, steamed with butter. If you're a gardener, pick the beans early, before the sun hits them.

Serves 4

1 lb	fresh green beans	500 g
2 tbsp	butter	30 mL
1/4 cup	water	50 mL
	salt and freshly ground pepper	

☐ Tail the beans and break into 2 inch (5 cm) lengths.

In a large frying pan, melt butter. Add beans and shake the pan briskly to turn them in the melted butter. Add water and cover tightly. Cook beans 7 to 9 minutes, or until just tender. Salt lightly and add freshly ground pepper. Serve immediately.

Cream Glazed Variation: Do not add water. When beans have cooked for 5 minutes in butter, remove cover and add 1/2 cup (125 mL) whipping cream. Cook, uncovered, stirring gently until cream has reduced to a glaze. Add salt, pepper, and a good bash of freshly chopped parsley. Serve at once.

Bacon Onion Variation: Omit the butter. Instead, put 2 slices of streaky bacon, finely diced, in the frying pan over medium heat. As soon as it begins to sizzle, add beans, water, and 2 green onions, diced. Cook as above.

Snap Bean Salad with Shallots and Herbs

Beans from the garden not only taste different than frozen beans – they feel different in your mouth. Only when the beans are garden fresh will you get the delicate flavor and crunchy baby-bean texture of this summer salad. Choose young slender beans and pick them early. Cook at once, before the sugar has time to convert to starch. The beans can then be refrigerated until you're ready to put the salad together. If you can't find shallots, substitute the white part of green onions.

Serves 4 to 6

2 cups	green beans, cut	500 mL
2 cups	yellow wax beans	500 mL
1	small sweet red pepper	1
3 or 4	shallots, thinly sliced	3 or 4
1/2 cup	low-fat yogurt	125 mL
1/3 cup	light mayonnaise	75 mL
2 tsp	deli-style grainy mustard	10 mL
1/4 cup	fresh chives, minced	50 mL
1/4 cup	fresh dillweed, minced	50 mL
	salt and pepper	

☐ Cook beans in lightly salted boiling water until just tender. Drain and refresh under cold water.

Seed pepper and cut in quarters, lengthwise. With a very sharp chef's knife, slice into finest possible julienne. (Some processors have a blade for a fine julienne.)

Put beans, pepper, and shallots into a salad bowl. Mix yogurt, mayonnaise, mustard, and herbs together, and pour over the vegetables. Add salt and pepper. Toss and taste a bean to correct the seasoning.

Terrine of Garbanzo Beans
with Vine Leaves

Like well-made meat terrines, vegetable terrines
have to have two things – a certain substance
and a good bash of flavor right off the top.

In this one, the substance comes from the meaty
texture of the garbanzo beans. The sassy whack
of flavor is provided by the garlic, lemon, and
dried chilies, which are a perfect foil for the
gentle bean-and-tahini base. The ivory-colored
terrine, studded with bits of bright color from the
carrot and onion and robed in the dark green
vine leaves, looks smashing served in slices as a
first course or as part of an antipasto. It's a
lovely, light dish to serve with drinks and
conversation on a warm summer night.

Surround the unmolded terrine with ripe olives,
small red radishes, cucumber, and lemon
wedges. Offer it with a basket of crusty bread,
homemade croutons, or warm pita bread.

Serves 8 to 10

■ *Note:* Tahini, or sesame seed paste, is available at gourmet counters, Middle Eastern or Greek grocers, health food shops, as well as most supermarkets.

2	19 oz (540 mL) cans water-pack garbanzos	2
2 tbsp	sesame paste (tahini)	30 mL
4	cloves garlic, pressed	4
1 tbsp	lemon juice	15 mL
3 tbsp	butter	45 mL
1	large carrot, finely diced	1
1	red onion, finely diced	1
1 tsp	dried chili peppers, crushed	5 mL
3	eggs, lightly beaten	3
1/2 cup	dry bread crumbs	125 mL
1 1/2 tsp	salt	7 mL
1 tsp	cracked black pepper	5 mL
1/2 cup	fresh parsley, chopped	125 mL
1 dozen	grapevine leaves in brine	1 dozen

☐ Drain the garbanzo beans. Place beans, tahini, pressed garlic, and lemon juice in a blender and puree. Pour into a medium bowl.

Melt butter in a small frying pan and add finely diced carrot, red onion, and crushed chili peppers. Fry briefly, about 3 minutes, until color of carrots intensifies and onion is transparent but not browned.

Add to pureed beans, along with eggs, bread crumbs, salt, cracked pepper, and parsley. (If you have no cracked black pepper, use coarse ground.)

Stir until well combined.

Coat a 9 x 5 inch (2 L) loaf pan with a non-stick spray. Cut a piece of waxed paper to fit the bottom and lay it in the pan. Spray again.

Rinse grapevine leaves and pat dry between paper towels. Line the pan with the leaves overlapping so all space is covered and the leaves overlap the edge. Spoon the bean mixture into the pan, smoothing the surface. Fold the overlapping vine leaves over the top, and finish with one or two additional leaves so the filling is completely enclosed.

Place the terrine in a larger pan on the lower rack of the oven. Pour hot water into the larger pan about halfway up the terrine. Bake at 375 F (190 C) for about 1 hour. Let the terrine rest about 15 minutes before turning out on a platter and garnishing. Serve warm, cool, or chilled. This slices best when cold. Use a sharp knife.

Chapter 5 ■ Bean Sprouts

IN THE MARKET: Almost any seed can be sprouted and then eaten in a salad, sandwich, or casserole. Look for clean, crisp sprouts with beans attached. Avoid the displays of broken, discolored, or shriveled sprouts with a lot of brown ends as they'll deteriorate quickly.

■ *Nutrition:* Bean sprouts are low in calories and a good source of vegetable protein.

■ *Season:* Year-round.

■ *Buy:* 4 oz (115 grams) per person.

IN THE KITCHEN: Refrigerate for up to 3 days in a plastic bag. Rinse before using.

*Bean Sprout Salad
with Fresh Ginger*

*Bean Sprouts with
Noodles and Lettuce,
Thai Style*

*Pot Stickers with
Bean Sprouts and
Sausage*

Thai Salad Rolls

Bean Sprout Salad with Fresh Ginger

A crunchy, zingy salad of the Korean persuasion, this simple side dish takes its vivid flavor from freshly grated ginger and its smoky undertone from a few drops of sesame oil.

Serves 4 to 6

4 cups	bean sprouts	1 L
2	green onions, julienne	2
1	large carrot, coarsely shredded	1
1 tsp	freshly grated ginger	5 mL
1 tsp	sugar	5 mL
3 tbsp	soy sauce	45 mL
4 tbsp	rice vinegar	60 mL
1 tsp	sesame oil	5 mL
	salt and pepper	

☐ Put fresh bean sprouts in a colander and blanch by pouring boiling water over them. Drain well.

Place drained sprouts in a salad bowl with green onions cut in long, fine julienne. Add coarsely grated carrot.

In a small bowl, stir together grated ginger, sugar, soy sauce, rice vinegar, and sesame oil. Drizzle over vegetables and toss. Let vegetables marinate in the sauce for at least an hour before serving. Season with salt and pepper.

Bean Sprouts with Noodles and Lettuce, Thai Style

Is it a warm salad or a pasta entrée? Whatever you decide, the combination of crunchy bean sprouts and warm, soft noodles with cold, crisp lettuce is an amazing dish. Romaine, iceberg lettuce, spinach, or a combination of all three work well here. It can be served alone or with a satay of pork or lamb. The recipe contains no salt because there is salt in the Thai peanut sauce and in the peanuts. Correct the seasoning to your taste.

Serve 6

1 1/2 cups	broken vermicelli	375 mL
2 cups	bean sprouts	500 mL
4	green onions, shredded	4
3 cups	lettuce, shredded	750 mL
1/4 cup	crushed salted peanuts, garnish	50 mL
	green onion and cilantro, garnish	

Thai Dressing

1/3 cup	Thai peanut sauce	75 mL
1 tbsp	canola oil	15 mL
1/2 tsp	sesame oil	2 mL
1 tbsp	rice vinegar	15 mL
1	small dried chili, crushed	1
1 or 2 tbsp	cilantro, minced	15 or 30 mL

☐ In a large pot of boiling water, cook vermicelli according to package directions. When the vermicelli is al dente (firm with some resistance or bite), drop bean sprouts into the pot and leave them for 30 seconds to blanch. Pour into a colander and refresh under cold water.

Put into a large glass bowl. Top with green onion and shredded lettuce.

To prepare the dressing, put peanut sauce, oil, rice vinegar, crushed chili, and cilantro in a jar and shake vigorously. Immediately pour over contents of bowl. Toss.

Serve on a large platter, garnished with crushed peanuts, green onion shreds, and wisps of cilantro.

Pot Stickers with Bean Sprouts and Sausage

Every Asian cuisine has its own version of filled dumplings, a sociable dish that often involves the whole family, assembly-line style, making hundreds of *jao-tze* with blinding speed. In the Muslim regions of China, Uygar men exhibit a fine blend of skill and sociability as they sit at outdoor tables, swatting flies and filling these dumplings with ground lamb laced with garlic. The next lamb to go is frequently tethered to somebody's chair. My pot stickers replace lamb with finely minced garlic sausage.

Pot stickers are traditionally browned on one side only, but browning both sides adds a toasted flavor and a slightly firmer texture that is delightful with the crunchy filling. Wonton skins (or gyoza wraps) are found in the refrigerated section of most markets. Rice sticks, or *mai fun,* are thin, rice-based noodles available in the pasta section of supermarkets or oriental markets.

Serve the dumplings as an appetizer, or add a salad and let these be the main course. Serve with a spicy dipping sauce or a saucer of black rice vinegar with a little fresh ginger grated into it.

(Continued on page 56)

Pot Stickers with Bean Sprouts and Sausage

(Continued from page 55)

Makes 2 dozen

1 cup	rice sticks, broken	250 mL
2 tsp	sesame oil	10 mL
2 cups	bean sprouts, chopped	500 mL
1/2 cup	radishes, finely diced	125 mL
1	green onion, finely minced	1
1/2 cup	red bell pepper, finely diced	125 mL
1/2 cup	garlic sausage, finely minced	125 mL
1	clove garlic, pressed	1
1 tsp	freshly grated ginger	5 mL
	salt and pepper	
2 tsp	cornstarch	10 mL
1/4 cup	cold water	50 mL
24	wonton skins	24
	canola oil	

☐ Cover rice sticks with warm water and let soak 5 minutes, or until pliable. There's a lot of variation among brands, so it's important to check after 5 minutes or nice firm noodles could become a glutinous mess. When soft but still firm, drain and chop.

Meanwhile, heat sesame oil in a large frying pan and quickly sauté bean sprouts, radish, onion, bell pepper, and sausage. Stir in garlic, ginger, salt, and pepper. Toss with rice sticks to complete the filling.

Mix cornstarch and water in a small dish. Arrange 6 wonton wrappers at a time in front of you. Place about 2 tsp (10 mL) of filling in the middle of each skin. Dip your finger in the cornstarch mixture and paint two adjoining edges of the wonton skin. Fold the skin on the diagonal, corner-to-corner, sealing firmly. (The cornstarch will act as glue.) Repeat procedure until filling is used up.

To cook, paint the bottom of a large cast-iron frying pan with oil. When hot, add the dumplings, fitting in only as many as it will hold without overlapping. Fry until they start to brown. Turn, let the other side brown, then pour in 1/2 cup (125 mL) cold water. Cover immediately. When the water has evaporated, the dumplings will be cooked.

To serve, arrange pot stickers on a plate with a small saucer of teriyaki dip or rice vinegar with ginger grated into it. Garnish with cilantro.

Shrimp Variation: Substitute 1/2 lb (200 g) chopped, cooked shrimp meat for the sausage.

Vegetarian Variation: Omit sausage. Add 1 cup (500 mL) grated mozzarella cheese to cooled filling.

Thai Salad Rolls

The soft, chewy texture of the rice paper wrapping is what many people like about these spicy rolls. Although most of us probably eat them as a walk-away lunch at a fast-food kiosk, they are delicious as an appetizer, and the filling can be varied to suit the season, the market, or your personal whim. Once rolled, they can be stored in the refrigerator for three days.

Salad rolls are everywhere, but the defining flavors in these come from the curried peanut sauce that goes into the roll. It's adapted from Menage à Trois, a two-person catering service with delightful food. I use Rose Brand rice paper, but any brand should work as well. Pickled ginger is a Japanese favorite, and it can be found in any oriental supermarket.

Makes 10 rolls

10	8 inch (20 cm) round rice paper wraps	10
20	cilantro leaves	20
20	spinach leaves	20
10	leaves of soft lettuce	10
10	long slices of pickled ginger	10
1 cup	bean sprouts, blanched	250 mL
1 cup	coarsely shredded carrot	250 mL
10	green onions	10

(Continued on page 58)

Thai Salad Rolls

(Continued from page 57)

Curried Peanut Sauce

1 tsp	vegetable oil	15 mL
1	medium onion, diced fine	1
3	cloves garlic, pressed	3
1 tbsp	curry paste	15 mL
1 tbsp	tomato paste	15 mL
1 cup	peanuts	250 mL
1 tsp	lemon juice	5 mL
1/2 tsp	salt	2 mL

☐ To make the sauce, put oil in a small saucepan and heat over medium heat. Add onion and garlic, and stir. Reduce heat to low. Cover and cook 5 to 7 minutes until onions are golden but not browned. Stir in the curry paste and tomato paste, and cook 1 minute. Remove from heat.

In a food processor, chop peanuts almost to a paste. Add curried onion mixture and continue to process until a thick puree forms. Scrape the puree into a small bowl. Season with lemon juice and salt. Reserve.

Soak rice paper wraps individually in hot water just until soft, about 30 seconds (this varies with the brand). Put the softened rice paper on a work surface and layer each with 2 cilantro leaves, 2 spinach leaves, and 1 soft lettuce leaf. Spread a generous teaspoon of the curried peanut sauce over the lettuce. Cover with pickled ginger, bean sprouts, and shredded carrot. Lay a green onion on top.

Roll snugly, moistening the top edge of the roll with a pastry brush so it will stick more easily. Store the rolls with this edge down. Serve with a dipping sauce of rice vinegar or Thai peanut sauce.

■ *Note:* If you want to be neat about this, trim the vegetables so that the ends can be tucked over and in, completely enclosing the filling.

Variations: The filling for these rolls is infinitely variable. Try cold shrimp or cold poached salmon with avocado and green onion. Long, thin strips of English cucumber and coarsely grated daikon radish also work well in these.

Chapter 6 ■ Beets

IN THE MARKET: In French markets on late summer mornings, vendors sell beets baked in their own skins.

Much as a baked potato has a fuller potato flavor, the baking of this root vegetable results in a richer, deeper, *beetier* flavor than the boiled version. It doesn't matter whether you use red beets, golden-orange beets, or the pretty Italian variety known as Chioggia with it's pinwheel striped flesh and remarkably sweet flavor.

■ *Nutrition:* High in potassium and vitamin C. Fair source of vitamin A. About 55 calories per cup (250 mL), cooked.

■ *Season:* Beets are available fresh, year-round, but only for a few weeks in early summer do we have the great pleasure of freshly pulled baby beets and their greens.

■ *Buy:* 1 medium beet per person, or 1 cup (250 mL) baby beets.

IN THE KITCHEN: To store fresh beets, clip the tops, leaving an inch (2.5 cm) of stem. Don't trim the roots or they'll bleed during cooking.

Fresh beets will keep well for a week, in a plastic bag, in the crisper.

To cook, scrub but do not peel. Leaving roots, stem, and peel intact during cooking prevents bleeding of colorful juices. Once cooked, the skins will slip off easily.

*Beets Baked
in Their Skins*

Spiced Baby Beets

Spiced Beet Salad

*Baby Beets with
Greens and New
Carrots*

Beets Baked in Their Skins

☐ Clip the tops leaving about 3 inches (7 cm), leave the root on, and brush beets well.

Place in a covered casserole. Do not add water. Bake at 350 F (180 C) until tender enough to pierce easily with a paring knife. Medium beets take about an hour, larger ones up to 1 1/2 hours.

Cool the beets and slip off skins under cold running water. The beets can now be used for salads, cooked dishes, or simply sliced and heated with salt, pepper, and butter. Squeeze fresh lemon juice over them, or add some snipped fresh dill and a spoonful of yogurt or sour cream.

Spiced Baby Beets

A Christmas Eve Reveillon is not complete without these beets to accompany the tourtiere. They're from an old family recipe, one that caused both my mother and grandmother a lot of trouble – their hands were always stained after peeling the beets.

The beets for this recipe should be smaller than a golf ball. Clip stems about 1 inch (2.5 cm) above top for cooking.

Makes 6 pints (3 liters)

30 to 36	baby beets	30 to 36
1 cup	white vinegar	250 mL
1/2 cup	cider vinegar	125 mL
1 cup	sugar	250 mL
3/4 cup	water	175 mL
2 tsp	pickling salt	10 mL
1 tsp	ground allspice	5 mL
1 tsp	ground ginger	5 mL
6	2 inch (5 cm) cinnamon sticks	6
18	whole cloves	18

☐ In a Dutch oven or stockpot, cook beets in boiling salted water until fork-tender, roughly 20 minutes. Drain, run cold water over them, slip off the skins, and trim tops.

In a medium pan, combine vinegars, sugar, water, salt, allspice, and ginger. Bring to a boil, reduce heat, and simmer 5 minutes.

Have ready 6 sterilized pint jars with sealer tops. Put a cinnamon stick and 3 whole cloves in each jar. Pack beets into jars. Pour hot syrup over beets to within 1/8 inch (2.5 mm) of the top. All beets must be completely covered in syrup. Seal immediately. Store in a cool, dark place about 1 month before using so the flavors will have time to ripen.

Spiced Beet Salad

A simple salad to make, and the bright ruby colors and sweet-spicy flavors in this dish will go well with almost any barbecued meat, baked salmon, or dark rye bread and grilled sausages.

Serves 8

4 cups	spiced beets in juice (see recipe above)	1 L
2	mild onions, Maui or Vidalia	2
	red leaf lettuce	
	chopped chives	
	sour cream or yogurt	

□ Peel onions and cut into generous slices. Separate into rings and lay in a bowl. Drain the syrup from the spiced beets over the onions.

Slice the beets over the onions. Cover snugly with plastic wrap and refrigerate for a few hours.

To serve, line a platter with red leaf lettuce. Arrange the sliced beets over the lettuce and distribute the onion rings randomly over the beets. Sprinkle with chopped chives and serve with sour cream or low-fat yogurt on the side.

Baby Beets with Greens and New Carrots

In early summer, my grandmother used to make this dish with a mixture of beet greens, spinach, and Swiss chard, and bake it for at least an hour with baby beets, carrots, and a bit of onion. Lots of butter, a drizzle of vinegar, and it was ready to eat. It looked ghastly, but it had a dark, earthy flavor that I adored.

I don't cook this dish as long as she did because I like the color and texture to stay. It is only possible in late June and July, when the fates conspire to have baby beets, tiny carrots, green onions, and fresh dill in the garden all at once.

Serves 4 to 6

12	baby beets with tops	12
12	baby carrots	12
2	green onions, chopped	2
2 tbsp	butter	30 mL
1/4 cup	fresh minced dillweed	50 mL
1	green onion, minced	1
1 tbsp	red wine vinegar	15 mL
1 tsp	sugar	5 mL
	salt and pepper	

☐ Scrub, but do not peel, about a dozen baby beets and carrots. Trim tops to about an inch (2.5 cm). Thoroughly wash beet greens to rid them of lingering bugs or sand.

Cover beets and carrots with cold water. Bring to a boil and cook until just tender.

Plunge beet greens briefly into the hot cooking water, just long enough to wilt them.

Lay greens in a lightly buttered oven-proof dish – a small platter or pie plate is ideal. Slip skins off beets. Distribute cooked beets and carrots on top. Sprinkle with chopped green onions. Cover and bake in a 325 F (160 C) oven about 15 minutes.

In a small pot, melt butter. Add freshly minced dillweed, minced green onion, vinegar, sugar, salt, and a good bash of freshly ground pepper. Bring to a simmer.

Remove dish from oven and drizzle with sauce. Serve at once, with sour cream or yogurt on the side.

Chapter 3 ■ Broccoli

ONCE AGAIN, THE ITALIANS LED THE WAY FROM THE GARDEN TO THE table. They had at least one variety of broccoli all to themselves from the time of ancient Rome, but it didn't reach France until that enterprising little woman Catherine de Medici took it along to her new home (along with, it seems, half the cooks and most of the good recipes in Italy). From that point on, the French court and all its hangers-on loved broccoli, or at least pretended to.

It's not surprising that when broccoli finally appeared on North American tables, it came, once again, from Italian farmers who emigrated to California, where most of the commercial crop is now produced.

IN THE MARKET: Broccoli growers deal in dozens of varieties of this nutritious vegetable, and they seem to specialize in strong, intimidating names: Green Valiant, Emperor, Saga, Everest, Goliath, and Paragon.

Look for firm, crisp plants with deep color. The florets at the top should be tight clusters of tiny buds, dark green to almost purple, carried on slender, pale green stems. If the stems are too thick, they'll be fibrous and woody; if the buds are turning yellow or beginning to flower, they'll be bitter. With broccoli, youth is all.

There are new varieties popping up yearly, like the Romanesco broccoli sometimes called broccoflower. Then there's broccoli raab, an Italian broccoli with loose heads and a distinctive, mustardy bite to the flavor.

■ *Season:* Local broccoli appears in late summer. Commercially, it peaks from October through Christmas but is available all year. Due to long storage, commercial broccoli is less sweet and flavorful than that from a local garden.

■ *Nutrition:* Excellent source of calcium and vitamins A and C. Believed to be an important part of an anti-cancer diet. 40 calories per cup (250 mL), cooked.

Baked Broccoli Omelet with Tomatoes and Cheese

Marinated Broccoli Stems with Ripe Olives

Stir-Fried Broccoli, Sweet and Hot

Twice-Cooked Broccoli with Prosciutto, Tuscan Style

 *from The Garden*

■ ***Buy:*** 1 medium stalk per person.

IN THE KITCHEN: The thing to do with fresh broccoli is wash it well, clip off the tough end of the stem, peel the stalk, and it's ready to go. Or store in plastic, refrigerated, up to 5 days.

Cook stems and tops separately if you wish, but don't consign the stems to the garbage bin. They're crisp and mild, perfect for eating raw with a dip or lightly cooked and served with a simple sauce of fresh lemon juice and melted butter.

Baked Broccoli Omelet with Tomatoes and Cheese

Although much like a frittata, this dish has a more delicate omelet texture. Choose young broccoli on slender stems so the flavor of the vegetable will be mild and sweet. It won't require a long cooking time. Blanching, then a brief time in the oven while the omelet bakes, will leave the florets on the tender side of crisp. Serve with a stack of buttered multi-grain bread.

Serves 6

2 cups	broccoli florets and stems	500 mL
12	eggs	12
1	small onion, minced	1
1	clove garlic, pressed	1
1/2 cup	Cheddar cheese, grated	125 mL
	salt and pepper	
1/2 cup	fresh bread crumbs	125 mL
2 or 3	Roma tomatoes, sliced	2 or 3
	freshly grated Parmesan	

☐ Preheat oven to 325 F (160 C).

If the broccoli stems are at all thick, peel with a vegetable parer. Cut broccoli into bite-sized pieces.

Blanch the broccoli by immersing it in boiling water for 30 seconds. The color will turn a brilliant jade green.

Lay broccoli in a large pie plate or shallow casserole that has been sprayed with non-stick coating.

Beat eggs lightly. Stir in onion, garlic, Cheddar, salt, pepper, and bread crumbs. Pour over broccoli. Arrange sliced tomatoes on top and sprinkle with Parmesan.

Bake, uncovered, for about 25 minutes, or until set.

 *from The Garden*

Marinated Broccoli Stems with Ripe Olives

Broccoli stems are sweet, crisp, crunchy, and frequently forgotten, entombed in a plastic bag and left to languish until the next time the refrigerator is cleaned. Then, into the garbage.

It's a great pity, that. Broccoli stems have a mild, sweet flavor and delightful crunch, not to mention their low calorie, high nutrient content.

The original point of this recipe was to rescue and use the abandoned stems, but it's well worth doing for its own sake. It keeps well in the refrigerator for three or four days, with the flavor of the marinade growing more intense as it penetrates the vegetable. Broccoli stems travel well and make a nice option to the ubiquitous carrot sticks for brown baggers.

Amounts aren't critical. Simply use as many stems as you have, marinate them for a few hours, and serve them forth.

Serves 6

2	bunches broccoli stems	2
1/2 cup	vinegar	125 mL
1/2 cup	water	125 mL
1 tsp	sugar	5 mL
3 inches	stick cinnamon	7.5 cm
1 tsp	pickling spice	5 mL
1	small dried chili	1
2 tbsp	olive oil	30 mL
1 cup	black olives	250 mL

☐ Peel broccoli stems and cut into slender wands about 3 inches (7.5 cm) long. Place in a flat glass dish. In a small pot, heat together vinegar, water, sugar, stick cinnamon, pickling spice, chili, and olive oil. As soon as it boils, pour the mixture over the broccoli stems. Let everything marinate for about an hour at room temperature, then add the olives. Chill until ready to serve.

Stir-Fried Broccoli, Sweet and Hot

A fast stir-fry with brilliant color and sharp clear flavors, this dish is best made with young, tender broccoli.

Serves 6

1 tsp	dried chili pepper, crushed	5 mL
2 tbsp	sugar	30 mL
2 tbsp	rice vinegar	30 mL
1 tbsp	soy sauce	15 mL
2 lbs	broccoli	1 kg
1	sweet red pepper	1
2 tbsp	olive oil	30 mL
1	clove garlic, halved	1

☐ In a small cup, combine chili pepper, sugar, rice vinegar, and soy sauce. Reserve.

Cut off broccoli tops and separate into bite-size pieces. Peel broccoli stems and cut into bite-sized chunks. Cut bell pepper into slivers.

In a large frying pan, heat olive oil and fry the cut clove of garlic briefly, until golden, just to flavor the oil. Remove garlic.

Add broccoli and red peppers. Stir-fry quickly until broccoli is brilliant green and still very crisp. Pour vinegar mixture over vegetables and quickly toss to distribute the flavors.

Serve immediately on a warm platter over rice or pasta.

Seafood Variation: When the oil is hot, fry 16 large, peeled, deveined shrimp. As soon as they begin to turn pink, add broccoli and proceed as above.

Blackbean Sauce Variation: Omit sugar, rice vinegar, and soy sauce. Instead, pour 2 tbsp (30 mL) blackbean sauce over the broccoli as soon as it turns brilliant green. Stir-fry quickly and serve over steamed rice.

Twice-Cooked Broccoli with Prosciutto, Tuscan Style

This is one of the few dishes that works well with very mature broccoli or even leftover broccoli. The combination of first steaming it and then cooking it in hot oil brings out mellow, nutty flavors that go so well with cold weather. Maybe that's why I have trouble leaving garlic out of this dish and do, in fact, throw in a clove, well minced, about half the time.

Serve on toasted English muffins, topped with a softly poached egg. The egg yolk, seasoned with only a bit of salt and pepper, will flow into the broccoli and make a simple, delicious sauce. (A famous chef in Lyon, France, makes this same dish with cabbage instead of broccoli and substitutes a few shreds of smoked salmon for the prosciutto. The broccoli version is *infinitely* better.)

■ **Note:** Everything in this dish – toast, broccoli, egg – must be served screamin' hot.

Serves 4

1 lb	broccoli	500 g
1 tbsp	olive oil	15 mL
3 tbsp	butter	45 mL
5 or 6	slices prosciutto, shredded	5 or 6
1/2 cup	freshly grated Parmesan	125 mL
4	English muffins, sliced and toasted	4
4	softly poached eggs	4
1	clove garlic (optional)	1

☐ Cut broccoli into bite-size pieces and steam until tender. (If using leftover broccoli, omit this step.)

In a large frying pan, heat olive oil and butter until butter begins to foam. Add prosciutto and broccoli, and cook, stirring, over medium heat until the vegetable absorbs the butter and oil, and turns a light toasty brown. This may take 15 or more minutes because, for once, you want the broccoli so thoroughly cooked that it will almost melt into the butter, becoming an integral element of the sauce. Sprinkle with Parmesan and run under the broiler briefly, until the cheese takes on a golden-brown color.

Meanwhile, toast the muffins and poach the eggs. To finish the dish, spoon the broccoli-prosciutto mixture over the muffins. Top each with a poached egg. Grind fresh pepper over eggs.

■ **Note for garlic lovers:** This dish will not suffer at all if, when the prosciutto is added, you also press a nice fat clove of garlic into the foaming butter.

Chapter 8 ■ Brussel Sprouts

IN THE MARKET: Brussel sprouts are surely one of the prettiest vegetables in the garden. Although we commonly find the green ones in the markets, they do come in two colors: the familiar green and a lovely red shade. Named Rubine Red, these blushing sprouts looks like miniature purple cabbages. Whatever their color, brussel sprouts grow in handsome columns along a tall stem.

Unhappily, fresh, commercially grown sprouts often disappoint, being unbearably strong and bitter. Look for sprouts at your local farmers market. They'll be fresher and more likely grown for their flavor rather than their shelf life. Once again, youth is everything – the older the sprout, the stronger the flavor.

■ *Nutrition:* High in vitamin C plus good amounts of vitamin A and minerals. 40 calories per cup (250 mL), cooked.

■ *Season:* Look for local sprouts from early September through late autumn. In some markets, you'll find them until late February.

■ *Buy:* About 4 oz (115 grams) per person.

IN THE KITCHEN: Refrigerate sprouts in a plastic bag for 3 to 4 days. Whatever cooking method you use, aim for less cooking time rather than more so the sulfurous smell that many people dislike has no chance to develop.

Marinated Baby Sprouts

Sprout Leaves Tossed with Bacon and Tomatoes

Marinated Baby Sprouts

☐ No recipe needed for these – just steam sprouts until tender-crisp, and while still warm, toss them with your favorite marinade or vinaigrette. Let the sprouts rest several hours or overnight. If sprouts are large, halve them before cooking.

This makes a delicious salad or hors d'oeuvre, alone or in combination with other vegetables such as halved cherry tomatoes or cubes of red, yellow, and/or purple bell pepper in an antipasto table.

A soy sauce-based vinaigrette is especially good with sprouts, bringing out a subtle, nutty flavor. A dill-infused vinegar, slightly sweetened, is also delicious with brussel sprouts.

Sprout Leaves Tossed with Bacon and Tomatoes

Separating the leaves of these tiny cabbages takes a bit of time but produces a dish of entirely different character. The tomatoes should be fairly firm, even slightly underripe, so they'll retain their texture during the cooking.

Serves 6 to 8

2 lbs	large brussel sprouts	1 kg
4	slices bacon, diced	4
1	large onion, diced	1
2	tomatoes, peeled and diced	2
1 tbsp	sugar	15 mL
1/4 cup	rice vinegar	50 mL
	salt and pepper	

☐ Cut bottom off sprouts. Blanch in boiling water 5 minutes, just so leaves are pliable. Separate leaves from sprouts and set aside.

In a large frying pan, cook bacon and onion until bacon fat is transparent and most of it is rendered out. Add tomatoes, sugar, and vinegar, and stir briefly. Add sprout leaves and stir-fry-toss until leaves are lightly colored. Turn heat down, cover, and cook about 10 minutes, until tender but not mushy. Serve with any pasta or rice dish, or with grilled sausages and boiled potatoes. Salt and pepper to taste.

Savoy or Napa Cabbage Variation: Roughly tear the leaves of a small Savoy or Napa cabbage. Blanch in boiling water to wilt. Proceed as above with bacon, tomatoes, sugar, and vinegar.

Chapter 9 ■ Cabbage

IT TICKLES ME TO THINK THAT WHEN CAESAR INVADED BRITAIN, HE likely had a cabbage in his lunch bag. Even before Caesar's time, circa 1000 b.c., the Chinese were touting cabbage as a sure cure for impotence. And in 1541 when Jacques Cartier made his third voyage to Canada, he brought with him a handful of cabbage seeds, which not only survived in that harsh climate but did wonderfully well.

Cabbage flourished wherever it was planted in North America, and a good thing it was because virtually every immigrant cook, from no matter what part of the world she or he came, had a couple of cabbage recipes up her sleeve. Ukrainian tables without cabbage rolls? German tables without sauerkraut? Unthinkable!

When I was a kid, there were many vegetables I didn't know or understand such as eggplant and fiddleheads.

What I knew, understood, and loved was cabbage. Every garden had some. It's a sad commentary on our value system that cabbage, among the entire vegetable kingdom, gets the least respect. Even garlic, which can be smelly and obnoxious if not treated well, has higher social standing, having achieved stardom at the hands of chi-chi chefs who wished to prove to the world how honestly earthy they'd become by concocting god-awful things like garlic ice cream.

Personally, I blame the cabbage problem on bad cooks. There have always been some who thoughtlessly hack a cabbage to bits, plop it in a cauldron of water, and boil it until it's limp and grey. The resulting mess has a powerful, sulfurous odor and is inedible. Thus we have a long parade of grade-B detective novels that begin, "The hallway was dingy, and it reeked of boiled cabbage . . . " as though cabbage is the culprit.

Winter Cabbage with Sausage and Root Vegetables

Red Cabbage Braised with Apples and Red Wine

Whole Stuffed Cabbage, Alsace Style

Cabbage Borscht with Lemon, Deli Style

Piffle. Cabbage is a great vegetable. The good cook stir-fries, braises, or steams it; or sometimes stuffs it, drizzling the round, firm, fully-packed head with cream and dill.

IN THE MARKET: The many varieties of cabbage fall into two main categories: round or ball cabbage, and loose head or oriental. Look for firm, unwilted leaves with a healthy smell and no discoloration.

■ *Roundhead:* Among the round types are the sturdy white and bluey-green heads, and the beautiful reds. First of the summer season is green cabbage, a soft, bright green head with a slightly conical top and mild, sweet flavor that makes excellent coleslaw. It's also fine stir-fried, or steamed and slathered with lashings of melted butter. Dutch or white cabbage is a larger head, tight and heavy. It makes excellent sauerkraut and is fine for soups, stews, or winter slaw. Savoy cabbage is the elegantly puckered, soft-leaf aristocrat of the cabbage world with a mild flavor and large, pliable leaves that are fine for stuffing. Red cabbage is the vigorously flamboyant vegetable that takes so well to braising with a splash of red wine, a little brown sugar, and a few juniper berries. If you have an in with a cabbage grower, ask for Scarlet O'Hara or Regal Red.

■ *Oriental:* These cabbages have loose leaves with a softer texture resembling lettuce, and a peppery-mustardy flavor that goes well in salads or stir-fries. *Bok choi* (thick white stalks and dark green leaves, sometimes called Chinese chard or chard cabbage) and the smaller *mei quing choi* (also called baby bok choi) both fall into this group, as does a relative newcomer to North American markets, *tat-soi. Tat-soi,* which I've also heard called black cabbage, has dark green, spoon-shaped leaves, which are shiny and crunchy. It goes well in salads or steamed with olive oil and butter. It's superb in a stir-fry with garlic and fresh ginger, touched with soy sauce or a drop of sesame oil. Napa cabbage, also called Chinese or celery cabbage, or *suey choi,* has long, pale green leaves and a mild, sweet flavor that suits stir-fries.

■ *Nutrition:* Cabbage is a wonderful plant, believed to aid in preventing certain cancers. It's high in fiber, vitamin C (uncooked), and also contains B1 and many minerals. A cup (250 mL) of shredded cabbage has only 20 calories.

■ *Season:* Year-round.

■ *Buy:* Count on a fourth of a small head per person, or 1 cup (250 mL) finely shredded.

IN THE KITCHEN: Roundheads take well to cold storage and will keep easily in the crisper for a week or two. Oriental cabbages will keep about 5 days.

Cut off bottom of core. Discard outside leaves if cabbage shows signs of wilt. Wash in cold water, cut in half, and proceed with the recipe.

Winter Cabbage with Sausage and Root Vegetables

This is a little like a *choucroute garni,* but it replaces the sauerkraut with wedges of fresh cabbage. You need a well-made sausage with lots of lean pork and a minimum of fat and filler. It should be coarse, liberally laced with garlic, and rather heavily smoked. A great meal for a winter evening with a loaf of fresh bread and some cold beer.

Although the recipe calls for a little wine or apple juice, it's an option. If your cupboard is bare, forget the wine and apple juice, and use water only – there's already plenty of flavor to go around.

Serves 4

1	medium head green cabbage, wedged	1
4	red potatoes, scrubbed	4
4	carrots, peeled	4
1	ring coarse garlic sausage	1
1/4 cup	dry white wine or apple juice	50 mL
1/2 cup	water	125 mL
	Dijon mustard	

☐ Cut cabbage into 8 wedges, trimming the core if it's large. Place cabbage wedges in the bottom of a 4 quart (4 L) Dutch oven or casserole. Quarter unpeeled potatoes and lay over cabbage. Halve carrots lengthwise, then crosswise, and add to the pot.

Holding the knife on the diagonal, cut sausage into 1/2 inch (1.25 cm) slices, exposing a maximum of surface. Lay them among the vegetables.

Drizzle vegetables with white wine or apple juice and water. Bake at 350 F (180 C) 45 minutes to 1 hour, or until vegetables are tender. Don't let them dry out – more water may be added if necessary.

To serve, arrange cabbage wedges in the center of a platter. Surround with potatoes, carrots, and sausage, and drizzle any remaining pot juices over the cabbage. Serve with Dijon mustard for the sausage.

Caraway Variation: If you enjoy the slight licorice flavor of caraway with cabbage, add 1/4 to 1/2 tsp (1.2 to 2 mL) of caraway seeds to the pot along with the wine or apple juice, bruising the seeds slightly first to release the aromatic oils.

Dill Variation: The same thing may be done with dill seeds.

Red Cabbage Braised with Apples and Red Wine

The next time you have a roast goose, duck, or venison, or even a mixed grill of sausages and chops, this is the dish to complement the dark, rich essence of such a meat.

By braising red cabbage, the brilliant color will hold while the flavors mellow and sweeten, and the apple literally melts into the sauce. I prefer the texture of a Red Delicious apple here, although almost any apple will do.

Serves 8

2 tsp	oil	10 mL
1	medium onion, diced	1
2 tsp	flour	10 mL
1/2 cup	red wine or grape juice	125 mL
1/4 cup	brown sugar	50 mL
1/4 cup	white or fruit vinegar	50 mL
2	large Red Delicious apples, diced	2
1	medium head red cabbage, coarsely shredded	1
	salt and pepper	

☐ Preheat oven to 350 F (180 C).

Heat oil in a 4 quart (4 L) Dutch oven.

Add onion and sprinkle with flour. Cook and stir while adding red wine, brown sugar, and vinegar.

Add apple and cabbage. Toss to mix. Cover and bake about 1 hour, or until cabbage is tender. Salt and pepper to taste.

Bacon Variation: If you enjoy the flavor of bacon with cabbage, use a slice or two in this dish, diced into the pot before you add the onion and apple. The smoky flavor of the bacon fat is especially good if you intend to serve the dish with wild game.

Whole Stuffed Cabbage, Alsace Style

The Ukrainian cooks of my prairie childhood were experts at stuffing cabbage leaves and rolling them into tight little bundles for the dish they call *holubtsi*. It was a lot more work than the equally good and, it seems to me, easier version – a whole cabbage, stuffed, as it's done in Alsace.

Cabbage rolls are often made with sour cabbage, but stuffing a whole, fresh cabbage with a meaty, spicy filling and serving it on a big platter surrounded by other vegetables (carrots, potatoes, small beets), turns this humble vegetable into a party piece, especially in late summer or early autumn. Serve it in wedges, accompanied by a spicy tomato sauce.

In winter, when appetites call for something meatier, surround the cabbage with boiled potatoes, carrots, and grilled chicken legs or a smoked pork butt, which has been baked and sliced.

A large, well-ruffled Savoy also makes a handsome presentation. Its leaves are agreeably pliable, but the procedure for stuffing is slightly different. See Savoy variation below.

Serves 6 to 8

1	large head green cabbage	1
1 lb	lean ground pork	500 g
1/2 lb	lean ground beef	250 g
1	medium onion, minced	1
1	clove garlic, pressed	
1 1/2	tsp salt	7 mL
1 tsp	pepper	5 mL
1/2 tsp ea	cloves and savory	2 mL ea
1 cup	soft bread crumbs	250 mL
1	egg, lightly beaten	1
1 cup	tomato juice or meat stock	250 mL

Spicy Tomato Sauce

1	19 oz (540 mL) can plum tomatoes	1
1/4 cup	brown sugar	50 mL
1/2 cup	medium hot salsa	125 mL
1 tbsp	cornstarch	15 mL

☐ Turn cabbage core-end up. With a short, sharp knife, carve away the core and inside of the cabbage, leaving a shell of about an inch (2.5 cm). Reserve the cabbage you've removed.

Place cabbage in a large Dutch oven or stock pot, hollow side up. Pour boiling water into the heart of the cabbage and around it to a depth of about 3 inches (7.5 cm). Cover and leave about 5 minutes. Remove and drain thoroughly. Remove two large outer leaves and reserve. Set head aside.

(Continued on page 76)

Whole Stuffed Cabbage, Alsace Style
(Continued from page 75)

Finely chop the cabbage you've removed from the head. In a large frying pan that has been lightly oiled, fry cabbage with the pork, beef, onion, and garlic. When onion is transparent and meat partly cooked, add seasonings. Pour into a bowl and mix with bread crumbs and lightly beaten egg.

Spoon stuffing into the hollowed cabbage, packing lightly. (Do not overpack or the cabbage may burst.) Cover stuffed end with reserved cabbage leaves and tie the cabbage with kitchen string.

Place stuffed cabbage core-end down in a large stock pot or Dutch oven, add tomato juice or meat stock, cover, and simmer about 40 minutes, or until cabbage is tender. Do not let it dry out.

To make sauce, break up tomatoes, mix all ingredients together in a medium pot, stirring until cornstarch is dissolved. Bring to a boil, reduce heat, and simmer, stirring until glossy and slightly thickened.

Remove cabbage to a large platter and let it rest 10 minutes for easier slicing. Remove strings. Meanwhile, add any juices from the cabbage pot to the tomato sauce. Surround the cabbage with cooked vegetables, drizzle a little sauce over the top, and slice into wedges, using a cake spatula to transfer wedges to plates.

Note: If you have leftover filling, it can be incorporated into the sauce, or made into a patty and cooked separately.

Savoy Variation: Use a large Savoy cabbage. Prepare the cabbage as above but leave about 2 inches (5 cm) of cabbage shell. Steam the head just until the leaves are pliable. Remove and reserve a large outer leaf. Drain and cool cabbage.

Turn the cabbage core-side up and fill the cavity with some stuffing. Cover the cavity with a reserved leaf. Turn cabbage over and gently separate the leaves into two layers. Stuff the inner layer, then the outer layer, reforming the cabbage as you go. Tie and cook as with green cabbage.

Cabbage Borscht with Lemon, Deli Style

This should be called Paula's Mom's cabbage borscht. Delis always have the best soups, and this one, which deli owner Paula Wiel got from her Mom, keeps the customers coming in the door at Hello Deli. Dry dillweed is suggested for a winter version of this hearty soup; in summer, use fresh dillweed and omit the smoked meats. This freezes well.

Serves 12 to 14

1 gallon	water	4 L
4 cups	canned crushed tomatoes	1 L
1	medium head green cabbage, coarsely chopped	1
1	large onion, chopped	1
2	large carrots, diced	2
1	lemon, juice and skin	1
1/4 cup	sugar	50 mL
3	tomatoes, peeled, diced	3
3 tbsp	dried dillweed	45 mL
1/4 cup	fresh parsley, minced	50 mL
	1 lb (500 g) mixed smoked meats: pastrami, Montreal smoked meat, corned beef *(optional)*	
	sour cream *(optional)*	

☐ Put water, canned tomatoes, cabbage, onion, carrot, and lemon juice and skin in a large stock pot. Bring to a simmer. Add the sugar and cook slowly for about 2 hours. If you wish to use the meats, chop them coarsely and add at the beginning of the cooking time.

Twenty minutes before serving, add fresh tomatoes, dill, and parsley, and continue simmering. Taste to correct seasonings. Serve with or without sour cream.

Beet Variation: To turn this soup into a traditional beet borscht, just add 4 cups (1 L) of diced, cooked beets (and their juice, if any). This will make a larger batch, which also freezes well.

Chapter 10 ■ Carrots

THERE WAS A TIME, AROUND 1600, WHEN CARROT TOPS WERE A European fashion statement. Smart women wore them to decorate fancy millinery, though I wonder how they kept the carrot fronds from going limp. I can't even keep them perky in water.

Carrots have suffered considerably in the intervening centuries. First came overenthusiastic mothers who fed them to us until we turned orange on the off chance that we'd be able to see in the dark and our hair would curl. Then came the frozen food artists who, modern science aside, still haven't managed to freeze a carrot without turning it into a cork.

Never mind. It's all in the past (except for the freezer corks). Here we go then. Carrots.

IN THE MARKET: The first sweet carrots of summer, bought from an organic gardener who pulls them at 6 a.m. and sells them to me at 8 a.m. from her stall in a farmers market, are one of the special treats of my summer Saturdays.

She grows the fat little French carrots called Planet and also Thumbelinas, shaped like golf balls with reddish-orange skin, plus several varieties of traditional Nantes; Clarion and Napoli are her favorites. She's so dedicated that she keeps a bag of them, scrubbed, as giveaways for kids who eat them like candy. Ed and I eat them on the way home and fight with the dogs over the leftovers.

■ *Nutrition:* Beta-carotene, a recent addition to the most-wanted list for healthy diets, is found abundantly in carrots. So is vitamin A. Carrots are also high in fiber, low in fat, and contain about 30 calories per medium carrot.

■ *Season:* All year – carrots are great keepers.

■ *Buy:* 1 large carrot produces about 1 cup (250 mL), shredded or finely diced.

Butter-Braised Carrots

Carrots Braised with Fennel and Parmesan Cheese

Carrot, Parsnip and Rutabaga Soup

Carrot Puree with Warm Indian Spices

Carrot Jalapeno Bread

Carrot Pudding with Two Sauces

 *from The Garden*

IN THE KITCHEN: Pretty as carrot tops are, they should be clipped as soon as possible as they sap the juices once you have them out of the ground. Refrigerate topped carrots in a plastic bag for 2 or 3 weeks.

When carrots are young and freshly picked, there is no need to peel them. Just scrub and eat, raw or cooked.

Food writers in search of a topic occasionally land on carrots with both feet, tossing into the carrot pot any old thing that comes across their line of vision. We end up with recipes advising of the addition of red wine, orange marmalade, blue cheese, garlic, spices. (I've even seen Kahlua added to carrots, God only knows why.) There are times when the addition of flavor elements is acceptable, even desirable, as in the warm, spicy dishes of the Indian subcontinent. But don't forget how good a plain carrot can be, all by itself with nothing but a good bash of butter and a speck of salt for company.

Butter-Braised Carrots

Braising is an excellent way to cook carrots of any age but is especially good for young, tender carrots as every bit of juice is retained while the carrot is encouraged to develop the fullest possible flavor and the generous blob of butter becomes a golden-orange sauce. These carrots are cooked with a bit of top still on them, partly for aesthetics, but also because the base of the carrot stem has an interesting flavor.

Choose a bunch of carrots that are about the length and thickness of your gloved fingers. Scrub them lightly, and get rid of the sand at the tops end, disturbing the tender skin as little as possible. Don't even *think* of peeling them.

Serves 4

1	bunch young carrots (about 16)	1
3 tbsp	butter	45 mL
1/2 tsp	sugar	2 mL
1/4 cup	water	50 mL
	fresh parsley *(optional)*	
	salt and pepper	

☐ Clip the tops of the carrots to about 1/2 inch (1.25 cm). Scrub gently and rinse thoroughly, being sure that no grit remains where the top joins the carrot.

In a medium pot, melt the butter. Add sugar and water. Bring to a simmer and add carrots. Cover and simmer about 15 minutes, checking to see that they don't dry out. Add a drop of water as necessary – this will depend to some extent on the variety and age of the carrots.

Continue cooking until carrots are tender (not tender-crisp, as in undercooked). If you like the flavor of parsley, add a good bash of it, freshly chopped, and a judicious amount of salt and pepper. Serve the carrots with their juices.

Carrots Braised with Fennel and Parmesan Cheese

Although Catherine de Medici would likely take credit for this dish if she could, it rightfully belongs with Lillianna, who could well be one of Catherine's descendants, considering her talent in the kitchen.

It's a winter dish. Use mature carrots and look for fat, firm bulbs of fennel with part of the feathery tops still intact. The long, slow cooking brings out maximum flavor in the older vegetables, and the anise-tasting fennel, which will almost melt into the sauce, complements it beautifully.

Be sure to use freshly grated cheese – if not Parmesan, then Asiago. There is a world of difference between freshly grated cheese and pre-grated cheese dust, from which all trace of honest flavor has long ago disappeared.

Serves 6

6	medium carrots	6
1	large fennel bulb	1
2 tbsp	butter	30 mL
3/4 cup	chicken stock	175 mL
1/2 cup	freshly grated Parmesan	125 mL
	salt and pepper	

☐ Peel carrots. Quarter them lengthwise and cut each length in half.

Trim fennel bulb, cutting off the root end and clipping the green top. If you wish, reserve some of the feathery fronds for garnish. Peel off the top layer of the bulb, which will be tough. Slice fennel lengthwise, at which point it will resemble a sliced celery heart.

In a large frying pan with lid, melt butter. Add carrots and fennel, and turn in the melted butter.

Add chicken stock and bring to an immediate boil. Cover, reduce heat to simmer, and cook about 15 minutes, until carrots are slightly tender. Remove lid and cook another 15 minutes or so, leaving the heat low and letting the vegetables brown slightly while reducing the juices to a glaze. Shake the pan to distribute glaze over all the vegetables. Sprinkle with freshly grated Parmesan, add a little salt and freshly grated pepper, and shake the pan again, using a back and forth motion. Serve hot, garnished with fennel fronds.

Celery Variation: Substitute a celery heart, sliced diagonally, for the fennel and proceed as above.

Carrot, Parsnip, and Rutabaga Soup

A simple puree of three compatible root vegetables laced with Jamaican jerk seasoning makes a superb soup for a cold night. I like to top this velvety, golden-orange soup with freshly toasted croutons that have been baked with a touch of garlic.

Serves 6

6 cups	chicken stock	1.5 L
4	large carrots, diced	4
1	small parsnip, diced	1
1	small rutabaga, diced	1
1	small onion, diced	1
1 tsp	salt	5 mL
2 tsp	Jamaican jerk seasoning	10 mL
1 tsp	lemon juice	5 mL

☐ Put the chicken stock in a large Dutch oven or stock pot and bring to a simmer. Add all vegetables and seasonings, except the lemon juice. Simmer for 30 minutes, until vegetables are soft. Add lemon juice.

Puree the soup in a blender in small batches, and taste to correct the seasoning. Return to the pot and keep warm until serving.

Serve in hot bowls, topped with freshly baked, garlic-butter croutons.

Celeriac Variation: Substitute celeriac (celery root) or salsify for the parsnip.

Kohlrabi Variation: Substitute kohlrabi for the rutabaga. Taste to correct the seasoning.

Carrot Puree
with Warm Indian Spices

Given their gorgeous color, you'd think carrots would evince more inspiration from the cook. In this dish, their natural sweetness is perfect for a puree spiked with traditional curry spices. Large, firm carrots work well here all through the winter. It's an especially good way to wake up the flavor in mature carrots that have been languishing in cold storage for some time. It's also a lovely dish with new carrots, when the flavors will be lighter and more elusive.

Serves 6

2 lbs	carrots	1 kg
2 tbsp	butter	30 mL
1 tsp	salt	5 mL
1/2 tsp ea	ground cumin, coriander, turmeric, cinnamon	2 mL ea
1 tsp	white pepper	5 mL
1	clove garlic, pressed	1
1/2 cup	skim milk yogurt	125 mL
	fresh cilantro, finely chopped	

☐ Peel carrots and cut into coins. Cover with water and bring to a boil. Cook until tender.

While carrots are cooking, melt butter in a saucepan. Add salt, spices, and garlic. Cook, stirring, for about 2 minutes. Turn off the heat.

Drain carrots, reserving 1/2 cup (125 mL) of cooking water. Transfer carrots and reserved cooking water to a food processor. Pour spiced butter mixture into the carrots and puree well.

Transfer carrots to a hot bowl. Swirl in the yogurt and a few finely chopped cilantro leaves.

Green Pea Variation: Fold 1 cup (250 mL) of tiny green peas, defrosted but not cooked, into the hot puree before adding the yogurt. The brilliant color and lovely poppy texture are a good contrast to the soft carrots.

Carrot Jalapeno Bread

Carrot bread isn't as sweet as carrot cake, but the spicy, moist texture and the tiny nuggets of jalapeno give it an elusive flavor and make it an excellent candidate for a cream cheese spread, glazed with either red or green jalapeno jelly. It's also a spectacular accompaniment to a vegetarian chili or a salad.

Makes 1 loaf

2	eggs	2
1/2 cup	sugar	125 mL
3/4 cup	canola oil	175 mL
1 1/2	cups flour	375 mL
1 tsp	soda	5 mL
2 tsp	baking powder	10 mL
1/2 tsp	cinnamon	2 mL
1/2 tsp	freshly grated nutmeg	2 mL
1 tsp	curry powder	5 mL
2	jalapeno peppers, seeded and minced	2
1 1/2 cups	grated carrots	375 mL

☐ Preheat oven to 350 F (180 C).

In a large bowl, beat eggs until thick. Gradually beat in sugar. Add oil and continue beating until smooth.

Sift together dry ingredients. Quickly stir into batter. Stir in jalapenos and carrots. Turn batter into a greased 8 x 4 inch (1.5 L) loaf pan. Let the dough rest in the pan 20 minutes before baking.

Bake for 1 hour. Cool 10 minutes in pan. Turn out and cool on wire rack.

■ *Note:* If fresh jalapenos aren't available, substitute two dried red chilies, seeded and crumbled.

Carrot Pudding with Two Sauces

1 cup	chopped suet	250 mL
1 cup	raisins	250 mL
1 cup	glazed fruit and peel	250 mL
2 cups	carrot, grated	500 mL
3/4 cup	brown sugar	175 mL
1/4 cup	molasses	50 mL
2 cups	flour, sifted	500 mL
1 tsp	cinnamon	5 mL
1/2 tsp ea	cloves and nutmeg	2 mL ea
1 tsp	baking soda	5 mL
1 tsp	salt	5 mL

☐ Stir suet, fruit, and carrots together. Add sugar and molasses. Sift together flour, spices, baking soda, and salt, and add to wet mixture. Beat well by hand. Spoon into a buttered, floured 4 cup (1 L) pudding mold, packing firmly. Cover with a lid or a well-buttered, double thickness of foil secured with an elastic band.

Place the mold in a large roaster or Dutch oven, and pour boiling water halfway up the side of the mold. Bring water to a boil and turn down to simmer. Steam pudding about 4 hours, or until it tests done. Serve hot with a sauceboat of Hot Rum Sauce and a dish of Brandied Hard Sauce.

Carrots and Christmas. Deprived of their beloved plum puddings, early prairie cooks, many of whom came from the British Isles, fell back on a steamed pudding that was quintessentially pioneer: carrot pud. Almost a glorified sausage with its abundance of fat, spices, and filler, the Christmas pudding made with carrots has become a staple for cooks throughout the prairies and the entire Midwest.

Hot Rum Sauce

Makes 2 1/2 cups (625 mL)

1 cup	brown sugar	250 mL
3/4 cup	corn syrup	175 mL
1/4 cup	butter	50 mL
1/4 cup	water	50 mL
1 to 2 tsp	rum extract	5 to 10 mL

☐ Put all ingredients except extract in a medium saucepan. Bring to a boil. Reduce heat to medium and cook until syrup forms a soft ball in a cold water test. Remove from heat and stir in rum extract. Serve hot.

Brandied Hard Sauce

Makes 2 cups (500 mL)

1/2 cup	butter	125 mL
1 1/2 cups	sifted brown sugar	375 mL
1 tsp	vanilla	5 mL
2 tbsp	brandy	30 mL

☐ With a small electric mixer, whip butter until smooth. Add sifted sugar and beat well. Add vanilla and brandy, and beat until blended and smooth.

Chapter 11 ■ Cauliflower

CAULIFLOWER IS ONE OF THOSE RARE VEGETABLES THAT MUST BE BABIED A bit as it grows. In order to keep the curds white, the leaves have to be gathered together and tied above the forming head to protect it from sunburn.

The earliest growers likely didn't bother tying the leaves, considering that cauliflower has graced the gardens of Asia for at least 2000 years and the ancient Asians had more pressing concerns than the color of their cauliflower curds. Cauliflower is still a big favorite in farmers markets from Kashgar to Delhi, and goes especially well in curries.

IN THE MARKET: Sadly, we've become so accustomed to the rubbery, sorry looking heads of supermarket cauliflower in their plastic shrouds that we forget the delicate flavor of freshly cut, creamy curds of a homegrown White Rock or a Snow Queen, either raw or briefly steamed.

If you have a chance to root through the cauliflower, look for firm, compact heads that are white or creamy, with no spreading. Avoid heads that are overmature with spreading florets as the flavor will be strong and the texture tough and stringy.

Cauliflower has a stylish new cousin, ranging in color from bright lime-green to purplish-green, known as green cauliflower or broccoflower. It can be used interchangeably with any cauliflower recipe. I've also sampled a purple cauliflower with delicate, broccolilike curds. Both cauliflower and its trendy relatives are delicious raw.

■ *Nutrition:* High in vitamin C and potassium, cauliflower is now considered to be a useful part of a cancer-prevention diet. Only 28 calories per cup (250 mL), cooked.

■ *Season:* Available year-round but peaks in local markets late summer through winter.

■ *Buy:* One medium-sized head for four people.

IN THE KITCHEN: Refrigerate in a plastic bag about 1 week.

Cauliflower Lemon Salad with Tomatoes and Olives

Cauliflower with Baked Tomato Rarebit

Cauliflower Tempura

Cauliflower Lemon Salad with Tomatoes and Olives

The contrasting colors in this marinated salad are wonderful for a buffet or in a picnic basket. So is the contrast in textures and flavors – the crisp bite of the cauliflower plays well against the soft, dark flesh of the olives, while their salty tang complements the acid of the tomatoes.

For the olives, choose a meaty, brine-cured variety from Italy or Spain. If you're growing Greek oregano, use it here, and try to find flat leaf parsley, if possible, as it tends to be more full-flavored than the curly variety. The salad keeps well for two days in the refrigerator.

Serves 6

1	medium head cauliflower, broken	1
1 cup	ripe olives	250 mL
2 cups	small cherry tomatoes	500 mL
1	clove garlic, pressed	1
1/2 cup	fruity olive oil	125 mL
1/4 cup	white vinegar	50 mL
	juice of 1 lemon	
1 tsp	dry mustard	5 mL
2 tsp	fresh oregano, minced	10 mL
	or	
1 tsp	dried oregano	5 mL
1/4 cup	fresh parsley, chopped	50 mL
	salt and pepper	
1	small lemon, thinly sliced	1
	fresh oregano leaves, garnish	

☐ Put cauliflower pieces in a bowl and pour boiling water over them. Let sit for about 5 minutes. Drain and place in a bowl with the ripe olives and cherry tomatoes.

Put remaining ingredients, except lemon slices and fresh oregano, in a jar and shake to combine. Pour over vegetables.

Put lemon slices in a small dish, pour boiling water over them, and let sit for 5 minutes. Drain and add to salad. Toss well to combine. Cover and refrigerate several hours before serving so flavors mellow. Garnish with fresh oregano leaves.

Salted Lemon Variation: Salted lemons are an Arabic specialty, a sort of pickle that is utterly delicious. Look for them in Middle Eastern specialty shops. Instead of the fresh lemon in this salad, add three or four salted lemons, cut into quarters.

Cauliflower with Baked Tomato Rarebit

A friend who was brought up by a British nanny remembers a simpler version of this. Nanny made a plain cheese sauce, poured it over an entire small, cooked cauliflower, and served it for nursery tea with toast soldiers. There are days when I could go for that.

I've taken liberties with Nanny's tea – my rarebit has chopped tomatoes, which improves it but takes nothing away from its homey comfort. Use the ripest tomatoes you can find for this dish. Serve it in soup plates, over slices of toasted French bread.

■ *Note:* The small amount of baking soda in this recipe prevents curdling of the sauce when the acidic tomatoes are added.

Serves 4

1	medium head cauliflower, broken and cooked	1
2	medium tomatoes, very ripe	2
1/2 tsp	sugar	2 mL
1/4 tsp ea	baking soda and salt	1 mL ea

Cheese Sauce

2 tbsp	butter	30 mL
2 tbsp	flour	30 mL
2 cups	hot milk	500 mL
1 cup	aged Cheddar cheese, grated	250 mL
1/2 cup	freshly grated Parmesan	125 mL
2 tsp	Dijon mustard	10 mL
1/4 cup	fresh parsley, minced	50 mL
	extra Parmesan	

☐ Put cooked cauliflower in a buttered casserole dish.

Blanch, peel, and coarsely dice tomatoes. Toss with sugar, baking soda, and salt.

To make sauce, melt butter in a medium pan, add flour, and stir until the butter is well absorbed and the flour cooked, about 3 minutes. Add hot milk, and stir with a wire whisk until sauce is smooth and thickened.

Whisk in both cheeses, mustard, and parsley. Bring to a simmer. Do not boil.

Stir in the tomatoes. Pour over cauliflower, sprinkle with extra Parmesan, and bake at 400 F (200 C) for about 10 minutes, or until golden. Yum.

Salsa Variation: If you're fond of spicy dishes with a bit of heat, add 1/4 cup (50 mL) hot salsa to this dish along with the tomatoes. Omit the Dijon mustard.

Cauliflower Tempura

The tempura batter is lightened with club soda or beer and crisped with the addition of cornstarch. The cauliflower is steamed briefly before dipping in the batter. This intensifies the flavor and tenderizes the vegetable without making it the least bit mushy. Many different vegetables may be used with the same batter, but I especially enjoy cauliflower.

Serves 4

1	medium head cauliflower	1
1/2 cup	flour	125 mL
1 tbsp	cornstarch	15 mL
1 tsp	baking powder	5 mL
1/2 tsp	salt	2 mL
1	egg white	1
1/4 cup	club soda or beer	50 mL
	canola oil for deep-frying	

▢ Break the cauliflower into florets and cut each one in half lengthwise. Steam briefly, about 3 minutes, or until barely tender. Refresh under cold water and drain thoroughly.

To make batter, sift flour, cornstarch, baking powder, and salt into a medium bowl. Whisk in egg white and club soda, and continue whisking until batter has the consistency of thick cream.

Pour canola oil into a wok to a depth of 1 1/2 inches (3.75 cm) in the middle and heat to 350 F (180 C).

Dip two or three florets into the batter, let the excess drip off, and slip them into the hot oil. Use kitchen tongs or a pair of cooking chopsticks to turn the florets once, and continue frying about 30 to 60 seconds, or until golden brown.

Drain on paper towels and keep warm in a 200 F (100 C) oven.

Serve with tempura sauce or black Chinese vinegar mixed half and half with plum sauce.

■ ***Note:*** Tempura sauce can be purchased at Oriental shops, any gourmet or specialty shops, or supermarkets.

Garden Patch Variation: Using the same batter, you can coat and deep-fry red radishes, short sections of green onion, slices of red, Spanish, or Maui onion, broccoli florets, carrot slices, zucchini slices. Fennel and squash are also wonderful in a tempura batter.

Chapter 12 ■ Celery and Celeriac

CELERY WAS KNOWN AND LOVED BY THE ANCIENT GREEKS, WHO valued it for medicinal rather than gastronomic use.

Eventually, the civilized world grew so fond of it that celery was part of every festive menu. It even had its own serving dish – a sort of vase – so it could come to the table upright, complete with leaves. Articles on good table manners carried detailed instructions on eating celery in polite company: how to deal with strings getting caught in your teeth and how to crunch like a lady.

Food scientists have paid little attention to celery because of its relatively low nutrient density, but today they're taking a second look with attention to possible preventative or even healing qualities.

IN THE MARKET: Although not widely grown in private gardens, you'll find both Pascal types (long green and loose) and Golden Heart (bleached, tight, usually sold as hearts) available year-round in supermarkets, and both are excellent. Pascal is fine for soups and stuffings, and the somewhat milder hearts are better for eating out of hand.

Celery has a faint flavor of anise, and is somewhat like fennel in flavor and texture, so it can be used interchangeably in almost every instance.

■ *Nutrition:* Less than 10 calories per stalk, celery is high in fiber, but low in other nutrients, although it does contain some vitamin A, B, and C.

■ *Season:* Year-round.

■ *Buy:* 1 large stalk will yield 1 cup (250 mL) of diced or sliced celery.

IN THE KITCHEN: Refrigerate unwashed celery in a plastic bag for up to 2 weeks. Once washed and cut, it can be kept in a plastic bag, refrigerated, for about 4 days.

Celery with Dilled Shrimp Stuffing

Celery Pilaf with Fragrant Spices

The crunch and the mild anise flavor of celery is important to so many dishes, but it's especially good in pilafs and stuffings.

Celeriac, which is a type of celery with a bulbous root that tastes much like celery heart, is a forbidding looking vegetable but easy to deal with once you make up your mind. Although European cooks, particularly Germans, seem to have a greater appreciation for it than we do, celeriac is gradually making inroads on buffet tables in North American restaurants.

Newer varieties such as Zwindra and Smooth Prague, have rid this vegetable of former faults: a nasty, gray-yellow discoloration inside and a pithy, woody texture. Zwindra is white, sweet, and crisp, but don't expect to find it in your supermarket. It's still a specialty variety, grown by dedicated and curious gardeners. Easier varieties to find in farmers markets are Prague and a small, compact root known as Brilliant.

As well as using it in several cooked dishes as indicated here, celeriac may be grated and folded into a good mayonnaise along with a chopped apple.

Celery with Dilled Shrimp Stuffing

I remember the New Year's Eve my mother discovered Cheez Whiz. She used it to stuff celery for an appetizer tray, and I was instantly hooked.

It took several years to get beyond Cheez Whiz, but eventually I found that Gorgonzola and Camembert mashed with toasted walnuts is a fabulous combination for stuffing celery.

Here's another one I like, using tangy feta cheese. Buy broken or salad shrimp for this – it's cheaper than whole baby shrimp and tastes just as good.

Makes about 2 cups (500 mL)

8 oz	feta cheese	250 mL
1/4 cup	mayonnaise	50 mL
1 tbsp	lemon juice	5 mL
2 tsp	dillweed, chopped	10 mL
1	green onion, minced	1
	dash hot pepper sauce	
1 cup	broken, cooked shrimp	250 mL
	celery sticks	

☐ Drain feta cheese. With a fork, mash cheese until smooth. Beat in mayonnaise, lemon juice, dillweed, onion, and hot pepper sauce. Fold in broken shrimp. Refrigerate until ready to stuff celery. Fill stalks generously with the mixture and serve with dark bread.

Cream Cheese Variation: Some people find the salty-sour flavor of feta cheese overwhelming. To make a milder version, substitute cream cheese and add 1/4 cup (50 mL) pimento-stuffed olives, finely minced.

Celery Pilaf with Fragrant Spices

Indian basmati rice is naturally fragrant with a grassy, leafy aroma that is enhanced by the addition of warm spices and the gentle anise flavor of Pascal celery. Be sure to use the leaves as well as the stalk as they intensify the flavor.

Plain long-grain rice may be substituted but will not have quite the same aroma and flavor. Thai rice, which has a faintly floral aroma, may also be used.

This pilaf is delicious with chicken or pork. If the chicken stock has been salted, do not add additional salt.

Serves 6

1 cup	basmati, Thai, or long grain rice	250 mL
1 tbsp ea	canola oil and butter	15 mL ea
3	stalks celery with leaves, diced	3
1	large apple, diced	1
1/2 cup	unblanched almonds, slivered	125 mL
1/2 tsp ea	cinnamon and allspice	2 mL ea
2 tsp	curry powder	10 mL
2 1/2 cups	chicken stock	625 mL
	salt *(optional)*	

☐ Rinse basmati rice thoroughly in cold water and drain in a sieve. If using long-grain rice instead, don't rinse.

In a large frying pan, heat oil and butter. Add rice and stir-fry until it is lightly toasted. Add celery, apple, almonds, and spices. Stir-fry about 3 minutes. Spoon into an 8 cup (2 L) casserole. Add chicken stock. Cover and bake in a 375 F (190 C) oven for about 35 minutes, or until rice is tender and liquid has been absorbed. Fluff with a fork to serve.

Chapter 13 ■ Corn

THERE USED TO BE AN OLD MAXIM: IF YOU WANT GOOD CORN, FIRST put the pot on to boil. *Then* pick the corn and race back to the pot, husking as you go.

There's reason behind the madness – at almost the instant corn is picked, certain enzymes kick in, rapidly converting the abundant, fragile sweetness of the sugar in the corn to starch.

If corn is picked in the early morning before the sun reaches it, or instantly cooled after picking, the enzymes' action will not be so speedily effective.

Corn has an interesting capacity to not only retain the sun's penetrating warmth within the cob, but to generate its own heat if given the opportunity. This is what happens when cobs are dumped into truck boxes, covered with a tarp, and left to swelter in the sun for hours or even days before the unwary consumer forks over the money for a few ears of *freshly picked* field corn.

The secret with corn is to prevent the critical enzymes from kicking in by picking it cool and keeping it cool. Large commercial producers who can afford to do so, will hydrocool corn with cold water before it goes to market.

IN THE MARKET: There are now three kinds of corn in the market: standard, sugar-enhanced, and super-sweet. The super-sweet (sometimes called *sweet gene*) varieties have the advantage of holding their sugar level, not just for hours, but for days.

However, the super-sweet varieties are almost too sweet for my taste and tend to be a little tough. They're the cobs you'll most likely find being sold from truck boxes and in some supermarkets, and while they will probably not be the corn you remember picking in grandma's garden, they're a passable alternative if you can't get to a farmers market or a pick-your-own garden.

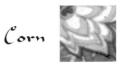

But it is those small sources you want to seek out. Corn growers who take their art seriously may trial five or six different varieties in a season, each with different qualities and wonderful names: Starstruck, Kiss 'n Tell, Buttervee, Peaches 'n Cream, Double Gem. Try the bicolors too, such as Skyline or Diablo.

■ ***Nutrition:*** Corn is a reasonable source of vitamin A and a good source of fiber. You're looking at about 80 calories per cob, before the butter.

■ ***Season:*** Sweet corn on the cob is available fresh in most parts of North America from May through October, and even later at supermarkets. Freshly picked corn is in season during August through mid-September.

■ ***Buy:*** Buy one to three cobs per person, depending on the size of the cobs and whether the corn is served as a side vegetable (in which case one small ear might suffice) or as a serious corn feed. A small ear of corn produces about 1/2 cup (125 mL) of kernels.

IN THE KITCHEN: Most corn people advocate leaving the husks on and wrapping in damp towels to keep the corn as cool as possible until ready for cooking. However, some local growers now tell me that in the interest of cooling corn as rapidly as possible, they strip it, plunge it into ice water, and then wrap it in damp paper towel and refrigerate. Either way, cook it as soon as possible after purchasing.

Corn on the cob is perfect when fresh and not overcooked, so here's how to do it if there's a garden handy.

Put the pot on to boil. Lots of water, no salt. Set the table. Have butter ready and a salt shaker on standby.

Off to the corn patch. Pick only the most perfect ears, pale yellow and juicy, the silk beginning to dry. (I like my corn on the young side.) Race back to the kitchen, husking as you go. Sounds familiar, doesn't it? Some things work so well, they don't need fixin'.

Now, into the pot. Lid on tight. Five minutes, that's all. Whiz, bang, finished. Out of the pot. Slosh of butter, speck of salt, let's eat.

Real Creamed Corn

The flavor and crunch of fresh raw corn, picked moments ago and still on the cob, is something everybody should try once on an early summer morning so they know what corn really tastes like. After that, they should try fresh creamed corn – one of the pure joys of summer. This can only be done successfully with the freshest, most tender kernels.

The number of cobs needed for this depends on their size, so just keep cutting the kernels off until you have enough.

Serves 4

2 tbsp	butter	30 mL
1 tbsp	flour	15 mL
1 cup	evaporated milk	250 mL
2 cups	fresh corn kernels	500 mL
1/4 tsp	freshly grated nutmeg	1.2 mL
	salt and pepper	

☐ In a medium saucepan, melt butter. When it foams, stir in flour and cook about 5 minutes over low heat. Raise heat to medium and stir with a wire whisk while slowly adding milk. Immediately add corn. Continue cooking and stirring until the sauce has thickened and the corn is barely cooked. Add nutmeg and salt and pepper.

Corn Salad with Black Beans and Red Peppers

You can make this salad with fresh corn in season, but it can also be made with canned kernel corn, and the canned black beans are also a handy shortcut. Take care to dice the red pepper about the same size as the corn and black beans.

Serves 6 to 8

1	14 oz (398 mL) can corn kernels	1
2 cups	cooked black beans, drained	500 mL
1	red onion, minced	1
1	small red bell pepper, minced	1
1	green jalapeno, finely minced	1
1/2 cup	cilantro, chopped	125 mL
3	cloves garlic, pressed	3
	juice and grated rind of 1 lime	
1 tsp	ground cumin	5 mL
2 tbsp	rice vinegar	30 mL
1/2 cup	olive oil	125 mL
	salt and pepper	

□ Place all ingredients in a large glass bowl or a glass jar. Toss to combine flavors. Refrigerate at least four hours before serving. Overnight is best.

■ *Note:* If using fresh corn kernels, stir-fry them briefly in very little oil before adding to the salad.

Polenta with Corn and Spicy Tomato Sauce

Now and then, for a family supper or a buffet, I like to do something in a ring mold the way my mother used to do it on Sundays.

Polenta is a good candidate. However, if you don't have a ring mold, or don't feel like looking for it, do this as the northern Italians do – simply spoon the polenta onto a platter and let it solidify a bit. Once firm, you can slice it and serve it hot as an accompaniment to any spicy winter stew or with a gutsy tomato sauce, as it's served here. Leftover polenta is wonderful sliced and grilled, either in a pan or over coals.

Most polenta is cooked in water, but this one is enriched with chicken stock and corn kernels.

Serves 8

5 cups	chicken stock	1.25 L
1 cup	yellow cornmeal	250 mL
1 tbsp	butter	15 mL
1	14 oz (398 mL) can corn kernels	1
2 cups	Spicy Tomato Sauce	500 mL

(see *Whole Stuffed Cabbage, Alsace Style* for recipe)

☐ In a large, heavy pot, bring chicken stock to a boil. Gradually sprinkle in the cornmeal, stirring as you do so. This is important to prevent lumps from forming.

As soon as it begins to bubble, reduce the heat and begin whisking with a wire balloon whisk. Cook slowly for about 45 minutes over the lowest possible heat, whisking vigorously every few minutes to ensure that it doesn't stick. When it's the consistency of cream-of-wheat, stir in the butter and corn kernels. The polenta is done when it begins to pull away from the side of the pan as you stir.

Pour it into a buttered, 6 cup (1.5 L) ring mold. Cover with waxed paper and let it stand for about 15 minutes, or until it firms up enough to be unmolded. Or just spoon it onto a deep platter – nobody will complain.

Serve with Spicy Tomato Sauce.

Jalapeno Variation: Stir about 1/2 cup (125 mL) of chopped, canned jalapenos into the polenta along with the corn. I often add a good bash of freshly chopped cilantro when making it this way. It can then be served with a pot of fairly spicy chili.

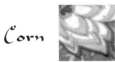

Sweet Corn Timbale

This timbale is denser than corn soufflé, more puddinglike, with a silky smooth custard enclosing the sweet little kernels. I like to make this in winter with canned or frozen white corn. The kernels are so small and tender they evoke the first cob of summer.

Serves 6

5	large eggs	5
1/2 tsp	dry mustard	2 mL
1 tbsp	butter, melted	15 mL
1/2 cup	soft bread crumbs	125 mL
1 cup	half-and-half cream	250 mL
1 tsp	salt	5 mL
1	14 oz (398 mL) can white corn kernels	1
1	green onion, minced	1
1/4 cup	fresh parsley, chopped	50 mL

☐ Spray a 6 cup (1.5 L) ring mold, timbale mold, or oven-proof dish with non-stick spray.

In a large bowl, beat together eggs, mustard, melted butter, bread crumbs, cream, and salt. Stir in drained corn kernels, onion, and parsley. (This can be done several hours ahead, covered and refrigerated.)

Preheat oven to 350 F (180 C). Pour corn mixture into prepared mold.

Set mold in a larger pan and add hot water to come halfway up sides. Bake for 30 minutes, then reduce the temperature to 325 F (160 C) for about 40 minutes, or until set. Let the timbale rest 15 minutes, then unmold on a platter. It will fall a little as it sets.

■ *Notes:* If you use a ring mold, fill the center with a complimentary vegetable such as glazed carrots, stir-fried asparagus, or sautéed cherry tomatoes. Otherwise, they can be scattered around the outside of the timbale to wreath it. This need not be unmolded; bake it in a casserole if you wish.

Spinach Variation: Line the mold with a double layer of spinach leaves that have been lightly wilted just enough to be pliable. Let the leaves overlap the top. Fill with corn mixture and fold leaves over it. Let set about 20 minutes before unmolding. To serve, use a very sharp knife and cut in wedges, or simply spoon off the servings.

Chapter 14 ■ Cucumbers

THERE'S A LOT OF ANCIENT CHARM IN A CUCUMBER. FOOD HISTORIANS trace them to early India, where their cool flesh must have been welcome on searing days. Some biblical scholars believe they go even further back, to the hanging gardens of Babylon. In fact, cucumbers were found throughout Asia and the Middle East where they are still an important part of the cuisine.

IN THE MARKET: Sadly, supermarket cucumbers are consistently disappointing. The glossy green field cucumbers we call slicers have been so overbred and overfed that they arrive in markets bland, full of seeds, and with such tough skin (heavily waxed or greased) that they would offend the average goat, much less please a cook in search of quality. Even the little Kirby pickling cucumbers are often bitter. Only the long hothouse varieties seem fit to eat.

Your best bet is to find a local grower who loves cucumbers, and then sample them all: long, seedless (or nearly so) English cucumbers, the slender, dark Japanese varieties, and the pale, curvaceous Armenians. Also try the fat little lemon cucumbers with their wonderful flavor and pale, smooth, edible skin, and locally-grown, bumpy-skinned Kirby picklers.

■ *Nutrition:* 1 large, unpeeled cucumber has around 50 calories and some vitamin A.

■ *Season:* Fresh cucumbers appear from June through September, with field and hothouse cukes available year-round.

■ *Buy:* 1 average cucumber serves 4; for the small Kirbies, allow 1 per person.

IN THE KITCHEN: Refrigerate in the crisper, or a plastic bag, for up to a week.

Cucumbers can be sautéed, grated for cold soups and sauces, or stuffed and baked.

Cucumbers with Ginger and Baby Shrimp

Cucumber Chips, Copenhagen Style

Cucumber Salad with Yogurt and Herbs

Cucumbers with Ginger and Baby Shrimp

The flavor and texture combinations in this Japanese salad are fresh and clean. Use thin-skinned seedless cucumbers such as the slender Japanese, the English, or the pale, curvy Armenians. Serve in small side dishes with a pasta or as part of an antipasto table. It's also good with buttered black bread, thinly sliced, or with grilled salmon.

Serves 8

1	long English or Armenian cucumber	1
1 cup	baby shrimp, cooked	250 mL
1/4 cup	white sugar	50 mL
1/2 cup	rice vinegar	125 mL
1/4 cup	water	50 mL
1 tbsp	soy sauce	15 mL
1 tsp	freshly grated ginger	5 mL
	salt and pepper	

☐ Cut cucumber in half lengthwise, then into thin slices. Do not peel. Put the slices in a glass bowl. Add shrimp.

Combine sugar, vinegar, water, soy sauce, and grated ginger in a small bowl. Stir until sugar has dissolved. Pour over shrimp and cucumber. Season lightly with salt and freshly ground pepper. Cover and chill well before serving.

Cucumber Chips, Copenhagen Style

More pickle than salad, these sweet-sour cucumbers are seasoned with dill. They need to marinate at least overnight in the refrigerator so the spices can do their magic. A platter of sweet-sour cucumber chips, liberally garnished with fresh dill fronds, is perfect with grilled salmon or skewers of grilled seafood.

Serves 10

2	long English or Armenian cucumbers	2
3/4 cup	white sugar	175 mL
1/2 cup	white vinegar	125 mL
1/4 cup	water	50 mL
1 tsp	pickling spice	5 mL
1 tsp	dill seed	5 mL
1 tbsp	salt	15 mL
	fresh dillweed	
	pepper	

☐ Thinly slice unpeeled cucumbers. Put in a glass bowl or large jar.

In a small pot, heat sugar, vinegar, water, and spices. Bring to a boil and pour over cucumbers. Grind pepper over them. Cool, cover, and let marinate in the refrigerator for several hours, preferably overnight, stirring occasionally.

Serve on a large platter, garnished with generous bouquets of dillweed.

Cucumber Salad with Yogurt and Herbs

This salad is the essence of summer, with its fresh, crisp textures and cool, green and white colors. There are two ways to make it.

■ If you want to serve it as a sliced cucumber salad with grilled meat, use one of the long, seedless varieties such as English or Armenian, or small, young, well-scrubbed Kirbies (pickling cucumbers) from a local grower. If using a Kirby, taste it first to be sure it isn't bitter. A little mayonnaise added to the yogurt sweetens and mellows the salad.

■ If it's to be eaten as a sauce, a dip for pita bread or other flatbreads, or as an accompaniment to spicy curries, it can be grated rather than sliced. I use plain yogurt without the addition of mayonnaise, and it becomes a *raita,* the classic accompaniment to curries, tandoori meats, and other Indian dishes. Use a seedless cucumber rather than Kirbies or the thick-skinned, seedy slicers. If all you have is a slicer, peel and seed it before slicing.

Serves 6

1	large English cucumber	1
	or	
3	young Kirbies	3
1 1/2 cups	yogurt	375 mL
1/2 cup	mayonnaise	125 mL
2 to 4 drops	hot pepper sauce	2 to 4 drops
1/2 tsp	ground cumin	2 mL
1	green onion, minced	1
2 tbsp	fresh parsley, chopped	30 mL
2 tbsp	cilantro, minced	30 mL
1 tsp	salt	5 mL

□ Wash but do not peel cucumber. Score rinds lengthwise with a fork. Halve lengthwise. Slice thinly. Put cucumbers in a glass serving bowl. Top with all remaining ingredients and toss well to combine. Let salad rest in refrigerator for about an hour before serving.

Raita Variation: Coarsely grate, rather than slice, the unpeeled cucumber and drain it in a colander, pressing firmly to remove excess liquid. Put cucumber in a glass bowl and combine with remaining ingredients, omitting mayonnaise. This is delicious when chilled thoroughly. Serve in small dishes with warm pita or nan breads, and grilled meats or a splendid curry.

Other Herbal Variations: Working with the same basic proportions of sliced cucumber, yogurt, and mayonnaise, or even omitting the mayonnaise, this dish is equally delicious with the addition of some chopped red onion, a pressed clove of garlic, and a good bash of fresh dillweed or snipped-fresh mint leaves.

Chapter 15 ■ Eggplant

A RELATIVE OF THE SINISTER DEADLY NIGHTSHADE, EGGPLANT GOT A bad rap from early European botanists who believed that it caused insanity. But in the Middle East they knew better and appreciated it for its sleek, buxom form, while using it in dozens of wonderful dishes.

Although we're accustomed to the fat, Italian, purple eggplant and the long, slender Japanese, there are dozens of other varieties that seldom get into supermarkets, but many of them can be found in oriental markets.

IN THE MARKET: Eggplants come in such a variety of sizes, shapes, and colors that keeping them straight is a challenge. Orange, green, purple, white, striped, lilac, blue-black; round, oblong, egg-shaped, berry-shaped, banana-shaped, and tomato-shaped. If that isn't enough variety to boggle the average cook, they also come in every size from berry-small to melon-large.

The oriental varieties such as Thai, Chinese white, Bitter Asian, and Japanese are usually less seedy than their larger European counterparts such as American or Italian globe, the Puerto Rican, Rayada, Casper, or Ronde de Valence.

Look for smooth, shiny eggplant with unblemished skin and a green stem cap with no trace of mold on the stem end.

■ *Nutrition:* Eggplant is a good source of complex carbohydrates and contains some fiber as well as vitamins A and B12. One cup (250 mL) of cooked eggplant, cubed, has about 40 calories.

■ *Season:* Year-round but peaks in summer.

■ *Buy:* 1 large eggplant is usually enough for four.

Grilled Eggplant with Asian Flavors

Grilled Ratatouille, Gypsy Style

The Easiest Eggplant

from The Garden

IN THE KITCHEN: Eggplant is occasionally bitter. It also absorbs a huge amount of oil during many of the traditional cooking methods. For both reasons, I pre-salt sliced eggplant about 30 minutes before using it, then rinse and pat dry. I also find that baking it in a little water first prevents some of the oil absorption when it is later grilled or fried, and also removes some of the bitterness that can ruin an eggplant dish.

Apart from occasional bitterness, eggplant has relatively little distinctive flavor. Rather, it provides an obliging background for other flavors.

But that's not to say that eggplant is boring – far from it. One of the best ways to prepare eggplant is to broil it, and when properly done, the meaty texture and mellow, smoky flavor will go well with almost any mixed grill.

Grilled Eggplant with Asian Flavors

The best eggplant for this dish is the long, slender Japanese variety, always available in Asian markets. But don't give up if you only have a globe eggplant; slice it crosswise and proceed with the recipe.

Serves 6

6	Japanese eggplants, halved lengthwise	6
1/4 cup	soy sauce	50 mL
1/4 cup	black rice vinegar	50 mL
2 tbsp	molasses	30 mL
2	cloves garlic, pressed	2
1 tbsp	sesame oil	15 mL
1/4 cup	canola oil	50 mL
1/4 cup	hot salsa	50 mL

☐ Score both sides of eggplant halves in a shallow cross-hatch pattern. Combine all remaining ingredients and pour into a shallow glass or plastic container. Lay eggplant halves in the mixture and marinate at room temperature for 2 to 3 hours, turning once.

Prepare a hot grill. Grill marinated eggplant skin-side down for about 5 minutes. Turn and grill 8 to 10 minutes, until well cooked. Brush with marinade. Serve with garlic-laced yogurt and any grilled meat. (See Grilled Asparagus with Herb Cream for yogurt recipe, adding garlic to taste.)

Zucchini, Onion, and Pepper Variation: To do an entire party platter on the same grill, double the amount of marinade and include zucchini, crookneck summer squash, thick-sliced onion, and sweet peppers. This makes a handsome party platter and is wonderful served with a cool sauce of garlic-laced yogurt.

Grilled Ratatouille, Gypsy Style

One of southern Europe's most sensually beautiful dishes, a well-made ratatouille presents an entire palette of vivid colors and lovely rounded shapes for the cook to enjoy when the creative urge hits. The finished dish is so aromatic and brims with so much flavor that it can stand alone, eaten with nothing more than some good crusty bread. Drink a young red wine, lightly chilled. Pure gypsy!

Although there are as many versions of this vegetable casserole as there are cooks, my favorite is from a cook in the Camargue region of southern France. He first grills all the vegetables over hot coals, allowing them to char slightly. It gives the dish a new dimension, very warm and earthy. A wisp of cinnamon enhances the tomato.

This is a perfect alfresco meal for a late supper on one of those heavenly June nights when you can't bear to go inside. Serve it at room temperature from a rough pottery casserole with crusty bread to sop up the juices and a plate of feta cheese, seasoned with lemon juice, olive oil, and oregano.

Baked Cheese Variation: If you want to serve the ratatouille hot, this is delicious with a layer of crumbled feta and grated mozzarella sprinkled over top before baking. Omit the lemon skin. Parmesan and bread crumbs can also be added.

Serves 8

1	eggplant	1
	olive oil	
1 or 2	large plump heads garlic	1 or 2
3	bell peppers, mixed colors	3
2	young zucchini	2
2	yellow summer squash	2
2	large onions	2
6	firm Roma tomatoes	6
	juice of 1 lemon, with skin	
1/2 tsp	cinnamon	2 mL
	fresh oregano	
	salt and pepper	

☐ Prepare a hot grill and put as many vegetables on at once as will comfortably fit. As vegetables are grilled, transfer them to a rimmed platter so none of the juices escape.

To prepare the vegetables:

■ Slice eggplant crosswise into 1/2 inch (1.25 cm) slices. Brush with oil and grill on both sides until well browned, turning once.

■ Cut a slice from the stem end of each garlic head and brush skin with oil. Grill about 30 minutes, turning once or twice, until garlic is soft.

■ Halve and seed peppers, and grill skin-side down until charred and blistered. Remove with tongs to a paper bag. Seal and leave 10 to 15 minutes so skin will steam. Rub skin off under cold running water.

■ Halve zucchini and yellow squash. Brush with olive oil and grill on both sides.

■ Cut root and stem off onions, cut in half crosswise, brush all over with oil, and grill until well browned on all surfaces.

■ Halve tomatoes lengthwise. Brush with oil and grill until lightly charred. Skin will split and can easily be removed when cool.

Coarsely dice all vegetables into a large casserole. Squeeze the garlic from the skins into the casserole – it will be soft and mellow. Stir in an extra 2 tbsp (30 mL) fruity olive oil and the juice of the lemon. Add lemon skins to the casserole. Add cinnamon and fresh oregano leaves, finely minced. (If fresh oregano is not available, use fresh parsley and dried oregano to taste.) Season with salt and pepper, and bake at 375 F (190 C) for about 20 minutes.

Let the casserole cool until it's barely warm to the touch before serving. Remove lemon skins. This dish can be refrigerated for up to two days – the natural juices of the vegetables will be even more concentrated and delicious.

The Easiest Eggplant

Such an easy dish hardly needs a recipe, but in case you might not have tried this dead-easy method of baking vegetables, here it is. The mayonnaise serves two purposes, being both a seasoning and a sealant, so the natural juices are retained during the baking. The best eggplants for this are the long Japanese ones, but the fat, purple, globe eggplants can also be used.

Serves 4

4	Japanese eggplants	4
	mayonnaise	
	freshly grated Parmesan or Asiago cheese	
	pepper to taste	

☐ Preheat oven to 375 F (190 C).

Cut the stem and cap off the eggplants, and halve, lengthwise. (If using the fat, globe eggplants, cut crosswise.) Cut a thin slice off the skin side so the eggplant will rest in the pan without falling over. Brush both sides liberally with mayonnaise. Generously sprinkle the cut side with freshly grated Asiago or Parmesan cheese. Grate a little pepper over the dish.

Bake eggplants until soft and the coating has browned, about 20 minutes. Serve with any grilled meat.

Chapter 16 ■ Fiddleheads

FIDDLEHEADS HAVE SOCIAL CLOUT. CONSIDER ANY OCCASION FOR which a chef from the eastern seaboard wishes to express a certain amount of national pride, especially if the guests hail from some distant shore. You'd think that for the vegetable course, a nice plate of baked beans or maybe a baked potato would be served.

But no. It's fiddleheads.

Never mind that a generous chunk of the population thinks a fiddlehead is the top end of a musical instrument, and another big chunk has never eaten a fiddlehead and doesn't wish to. Never mind that a fiddlehead's growing season is about 10 minutes long, and after that, the only way you'll get your teeth into one is to thaw it first.

Fiddleheads are not so much a vegetable as a symbol. Here in Canada, they're trotted out with maple sugar and the flag to celebrate the national palate, whatever that may be.

IN THE MARKET: These wild ferns appear briefly, usually in May, and often have a fair amount of flotsam and jetsam with them, bits of twig, etc., so they need careful picking over. The papery shroud still on the youngest ones can be removed by simply rubbing between your palms.

- ■ *Nutrition:* Contains some calcium and phosphorus. Low in calories.

- ■ *Season:* May

- ■ *Buy:* Count on 3 to 4 oz (about 115 grams) per person.

IN THE KITCHEN: Fiddleheads can be refrigerated, unwashed, in plastic, for about 3 days. Blanch 2 to 3 minutes for freezing.

*Sauté of Fiddleheads,
Radishes
and Green Onions*

Sauté of Fiddleheads, Radishes and Green Onions

If you want to use fresh fiddleheads, this dish is only possible for a few days in spring when the fiddleheads are just poking through the underbrush along the river. If you can't find fresh fiddleheads, use frozen ones, thawed under cold running water just until they can be separated. I use tiny red radishes, the smallest I can find, and the white part of the onions only. I like to use the multiplier onions from my own garden, which resemble tiny shallots.

When trimming radishes, leave a wisp of the smallest leaves on the end, if possible. During the brief stir-fry, the vegetables will release enough of their own juices to perfume the butter and form a delicate sauce.

Serves 6

3 tbsp	butter	45 mL
10 oz	fresh or frozen fiddleheads	280 g
24	small green onions, white part only	24
24	tiny red radishes, trimmed	24
	juice of 1 lemon	
1/2 cup	fresh parsley, minced	125 mL
	salt and freshly ground pepper	

☐ In a large frying pan, melt butter. Add fiddleheads and onions, and stir-fry quickly for about 3 minutes. Add radishes and continue to stir-fry. Radish color will immediately intensify. Cook no more than 3 minutes longer, just until radishes are hot through. Add lemon juice and parsley. Sprinkle with salt and freshly ground pepper, and serve immediately, drizzled with the pan juices.

Serve as a side dish with poached salmon and new potatoes. Drink a young, crisp white wine.

Cream Variation: If you can stand a few calories, remove vegetables to a hot dish with a slotted spoon. Omitting the lemon juice, add 3/4 cup (175 mL) of whipping cream to the pan, turn heat to high, and cook rapidly until it reduces slightly. Pour over vegetables.

Chapter 17 ■ Greens

LEAVING ASIDE THE SOFTER GREENS WE KNOW AS SALAD GREENS AND the firmer crowd we know as cabbage, there is a vast palate of leafy vegetables I call cooking greens. Not only are these greens typically loaded with nutrients, both vitamins and minerals, they're ridiculously low in calories and are fat-free. Quite beyond their extremely useful personality, when treated with the respect they deserve, greens lend themselves to the most delicious and artful dishes you could imagine. Although I like to cook this type of green, it isn't necessary.

■ **Beet Greens:** It's worth growing a few beets just for the greens. The flavor is unique among greens, and good Ukrainian cooks long ago learned to wrap the leaves around bland fillings such as rice or bread dough. They're also delicious steamed with butter or mixed with other greens.

■ **Oriental Greens:** Immigration from the Pacific Rim has introduced North Americans to a whole new range of greens such as water spinach, *mei quing choi,* and *tat-soi,* with flavors and textures that are delectable with garlic and ginger in steamed or stir-fried dishes. *Tat-soi* is also becoming a favorite salad green among chefs who have friends in the right gardens.

Many oriental markets don't bother with English signage on their vegetables but it's worth asking, and even if your English and their Chinese can't come to terms, it's worth taking some home and experimenting.

■ **Swiss Chard:** Both red and green chard were originally beets, but the botanical accent has fallen on their fleshy stems and lush foliage. In its raw state, the flavor of chard leaves has much in common with beet greens, while the stems have the texture, though not the flavor, of celery. Many cooks prefer to braise the stems and steam the leaves, but the leaves are also a natural wrap for vegetable terrines, rice rolls, or they can be used in combination with grape leaves to wrap cheese for grilling over hot coals.

Chapter 18 ■ Herbs

HERB USED TO BE THE NAME OF THE OLD GUY WHO LIVED DOWN OUR street. He was ninety-six and yelled at us when we cut through his yard on the way to school. That was about a century ago.

Herb was also another name for dill, which all gardeners grew in large quantities because prairie cooks couldn't make dill pickles without it.

One man and one plant. That was it for herbs. I've long wondered why.

Everybody else in the world knew all about herbs and always had. The culinary and professional use of these strange, wonderful plants goes back centuries, into biblical times.

Pesto for Hot Pasta

Focaccia with Summer Herbs

Most amazing of all are the wild herbs, those thousands of plants that you and I have probably never seen, let alone tasted. They grow in secret places and may even be magic, or so we're told. (Some people know a lot about these things.)

I have a vague childhood memory of an ancient, shrunken woman we called the Diamond Queen. She lived not far from us in a remote part of northern Manitoba with her equally ancient companion, Old Deaf Gilbert. In that part of the world, full names weren't used much. One name was really all you needed, so you tagged on a descriptor and away you went. Thus it was Dumas the Trapper or Freddie the Cook or Old Deaf Gilbert.

But the Diamond Queen's name didn't make much sense. Why wasn't she the Muskeg Queen, after the place she spent her summers picking things? Or maybe the Herb Queen, for the amazing stuff she harvested? Her name was a mystery, like her age.

One winter, some distant bureaucrat decided the Diamond Queen had reached 100. When a reporter wandered up to interview her, she informed him that she

was a heck of a lot older than that, and as she'd already outlived everybody who could have called her a liar, nobody felt qualified to argue. She told him why she'd lived so long, too. It was because of her magic medicine. Herbs, mostly.

Her log shack was full of smoky smells. There was the warm-sweet smell of wood smoke, the hungry-sweet smell of smoked fish and tanned deerskin, and the sleepy-sweet fragrance of whatever leaves she was using for pipe tobacco.

Her house had other smells – whiffs of licorice and wild onion, sweet berries and leaves. The Queen was a forager, and she knew everything there was to know about wild herbs and the things you could use them for. Women whispered that she could fix any problem, from getting rid of warts to ending an unwanted pregnancy. Men visited her, too, because she understood impotence, even if she didn't know the term. Jars of magic medicines lined her window sill, and whole dried plants hung by their roots from the roof beam.

Her garden was the muskeg where she gathered bear berries and juniper for making a bitter tea and something called solomon seal for curing coughs. Willow bark tea fixed headaches. The shiny, oval leaves that grew among the fallen pine needles were squaw vine and a spring tonic.

I decided that the Queen was a witch. I knew about Hansel and Gretel, and if the old girl had poked my ribs with her skinny finger and offered me gingerbread, I'd have asked which way to the cage. Her brews and potions, tinctures and teas, were no doubt medicinal. For all I know, they might have been magic. Nobody said they weren't.

Now is it *herb,* or is it *'erb?* This is an academic bugtussle very much of the *tomato-tomahto* genre. Let's agree to *herb* – we have the *h,* so we might as well use it. Now that that's settled, here are seven easy-to-grow kitchen herbs that give me the greatest pleasure as a gardener and cook.

■ ***Basil:*** Basil is my favorite of the aromatic herbs, whether it's the ruby-leafed opal, lemon, cinnamon, or Genoa basil – the list goes on. Its flavor is both spicy and sweet, with overtones of cinnamon, clove, lemon, even mint.

As early as 1400, Italian gardens overflowed with herbs, and sailors returning to Genoa always knew when they were close to home because the perfume of millions of basil plants wafted offshore from every garden along the Ligurian coast.

Basil and tomatoes are a natural marriage, but the classic use is in pesto. The pesto recipe below has flavors and aromas that enliven any pasta dish.

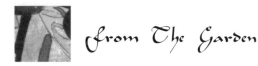

- **Chives:** Chives are the slender, delicate, mild cousins of the green onion and produce lovely purple flowers long before they're supposed to and then go to seed. The chive blossoms are entirely edible and make a lovely garnish for salads. They also go well in herbal vinegars.

Garlic chives are a flat-leaf version of chives with a more pungent flavor. Wonderful for salads and vinegars.

- **Cilantro** (alias coriander): Now a lesson in cilantro and coriander. *Cilantro* (sometimes wrongly dubbed coriander) is the leaf of the plant whose root is *coriander*. The two have different flavors and different uses. The seeds (also coriander, though some seed companies persist in calling them cilantro or Chinese parsley, just to confuse us) are sold as a spice. If you want to grow the stuff, it's a three-for-one deal: leaves, seeds, and roots, all edible. Can't miss.

Cilantro is my favorite Asian herb – I put a few cilantro leaves in chicken soup, use it lavishly in Thai chicken salads, toss handfuls of it in with pasta, and add it to many Mexican dishes, especially guacamole and salsa. The sweet citrus-nutmeg flavor of the seeds (referred to in this book as coriander) is indispensable in good curry mixtures.

Some people dislike cilantro because they find its flavor "soapy." I'm told that's because of the chemistry of their saliva. Thus I'm not quite so lavish with it when feeding strangers.

Buy cilantro in Asian markets with the roots still on – it lasts longer and retains far more flavor than the cuttings.

- **Dill:** Dill is a northern herb that has always perfumed the kitchens of eastern Europe, the Low Countries, and Scandinavia. In the market, look for the lush blue-green foliage of the dwarf dill called Fernleaf. It's coarser than ordinary bouquet dill, but you get more foliage for your money and more flavor. Wash it, wrap it in a damp paper towel, and keep it refrigerated in a plastic bag for three or four days.

Dill goes well with shrimp, cucumber, smoked salmon, lox, fresh tomatoes. I like it with green peas, and it's wonderful with tiny steamed potatoes. Use it in beet soup, tomato soup, or with carrots or artichokes.

- **Mint:** There are so many varieties of mint that you may be able to choose only absolute favorites for your garden. Use the leaves in iced tea, chopped into tabouli, or in a vinegar sauce. Even though it tries to take over, I love having mint in the garden – the dogs roll in it, the lawn mower bruises it, my careless feet squash it, and every time, it rewards us with a clean, fresh scent.

- **Oregano:** The word *oregano* is from the Greek *oros* for mountain and *ganos* for beauty. There are many varieties of oregano within the major European and Mexican strains commonly grown here. Look for true Greek oregano with its hint of sage and mint, and use it lavishly with tomato dishes, pork, rabbit, and chicken, especially when they're roasted or grilled. The delicate purple flowers can be used in salads, as a garnish, or to infuse oil or vinegar.

The ubiquitous greenish-gray dust that comes in tin cans or bottles and is sold as "pizza seasoning" is not oregano. Neither is much of what passes for oregano in the plant section of supermarkets, where I often find marjoram mislabeled as oregano.

■ ***Parsley:*** Winter or summer, I use parsley in so many dishes that I tend to take it for granted. Look for flat-leaf Italian parsley, which has a sweeter, more full-bodied flavor than the curly-leafed variety. However, for dishes such as tabouli or couscous salad, where a coarser texture is wanted, the curly parsley is best.

Because fresh parsley is so easy to find, I can think of no excuse for using dried parsley dust, which is the next thing to useless.

Pesto for Hot Pasta

Many cooks thump a lot of garlic into their pesto, but the best pesto requires infusing some extra-virgin olive oil with garlic at least a day ahead, producing a full, rounded flavor that complements the fresh basil perfectly.

Note that the fresh herbs are hand-minced, the cheese merely grated, not ground to dust, and the pine nuts not chopped at all. Unlike the blender versions of pesto sauce, this one will have more texture and flavor. If you can't find genuine Parmesan, Pedano or Asiago may be substituted. Taste the pine nuts to be sure they're fresh.

Makes about 3 cups (750 mL)

1 cup	garlic-infused olive oil	250 mL
2 cups	fresh basil leaves, packed	500 mL
1/2 cup	fresh parsley leaves, packed	125 mL
3/4 cup	toasted pine nuts	175 mL
1 1/2 cups	freshly grated Parmesan	375 mL
	salt and freshly ground pepper	

☐ Finely mince basil and parsley leaves, and put them in a bowl. Add the toasted pine nuts and cheese. Strain the garlic out of the olive oil and add the oil to the herb mixture, discarding the garlic. Season with salt and pepper. Stir well and pour over hot pasta. Toss and serve at once. Serves 4.

Frozen Pesto: Make this up in large batches and freeze in 1 cup (250 mL) servings. They'll be handy for pasta all winter long. Plastic freezer bags make convenient containers.

Focaccia with Summer Herbs

The wonderful flatbreads of southern Europe inspired this herbed focaccia, which is delicious with soup, as a snack or appetizer, or topped with tomatoes or cheese and grilled.

It can also be split horizontally while still warm, filled with thinly shaved ham and mozzarella, and put back in the oven (or on the grill) just until the cheese softens. Cut into diamonds or squares, and serve with a glass of wine to tide people over until dinner.

This recipe should serve as a basic flatbread, to be varied with additional (or different) herbs according to your own needs.

Makes 2 rounds

2 1/2 cups	all-purpose flour	625 mL
1 tsp	salt	5 mL
1	envelope quick-rise yeast	1
1/4 cup ea	parsley and chives, minced	50 mL ea
2 tbsp	fresh oregano, minced	30 mL
1	clove garlic, pressed	1
1 cup	water	250 mL
1/4 cup	olive oil	50 mL
	additional herbs and coarse salt	

☐ Reserve 3/4 cup (175 mL) flour from the total amount. Mix remaining flour, salt, yeast, herbs, and garlic in a large bowl.

Heat water and oil until hot to the touch, 125 F (55 C). Make a well in the flour mixture and stir in hot liquid, beating with a wooden spoon, gradually adding remaining flour until it forms a soft dough that leaves the sides of the bowl. If dough still seems too soft to handle, gradually add up to 1/2 cup (125 mL) additional flour. Turn dough onto a lightly floured board and knead until smooth and elastic, about 5 minutes. Cover and let rest 10 to 15 minutes.

Preheat oven to 450 F (230 C).

Cut dough in half and roll each to almost fill a 10 inch (30 cm) pizza pan, patting the dough with your hands to flatten it. With fingertips, make indents all over the dough. Sprinkle with olive oil and a few extra pinches of the herbs, very finely minced. Sprinkle lightly with coarse salt. Let dough rest 5 minutes, then bake about 20 minutes, or until golden brown.

Cheddar and Pepper Variation: Fold 1 cup (250 mL) diced, sautéed sweet peppers and 1 cup (250 mL) grated Cheddar cheese into the dough before kneading. Flour hands well to knead. Make a single round loaf, patted into the pizza tin by hand. Let rest 15 minutes in a warm place before baking.

Olive Variation: Before kneading, fold in 1/2 cup (125 mL) olives with pimento, or ripe black olives, roughly chopped.

Chapter 19 ■ Kale

KALE HAS NEVER BEEN AS POPULAR AS IT SHOULD BE IN NORTH
America. It takes a good Dutch or German cook to give this vegetable the
attention it deserves, pairing it with creamy cheese sauces, potatoes, and smoky
bacon or ham.

The dark, elegantly curled leaves of traditional kale have recently been joined
in the garden by delicate shades of red and lavender, and are being grown for
ornamental use as well as for their earthy, slightly bitter cabbage-to-broccoli
flavor.

IN THE MARKET: Kale is a member of the cabbage family, but it doesn't
bother to head. There are several varieties of kale on the market including red
Russian kale, which has flat, grey-green leaves with a saw-tooth edge; Dutch
Verdura, which has dark, blue-green leaves, thick and curly, with a sweet,
nutty flavor; and an Italian variety, Lacinato, with large, leathery leaves, a deep,
blue-green color, and intense flavor.

Some new varieties of ornamental kale are also edible, and their pretty pink
and purple ruffles have recently been adorning trendier salad plates.

■ *Nutrition:* High in iron, calcium, phosphorus, and vitamins A and C.

■ *Season:* This is a winter green that needs frost to bring out its sweetest
flavor. Look for it from January through late spring in supermarkets, late
September through November in local farmers markets.

■ *Buy:* One bunch of kale is usually enough for four.

IN THE KITCHEN: Store unwashed kale in a plastic bag in the refrigerator for
not more than two days. It wilts quickly.

*Gratin of Kale
with Potatoes,
Cheese and Bacon*

*Kale Soup with
Sausage, Lisbon Style*

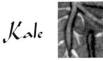

Gratin of Kale with Potatoes, Cheese, and Bacon

A grumpy, red-faced woman in the cafeteria of Frankfurt's railway station doles a version of this out to hungry travelers. I don't pretend to have her recipe, but it's close. Combining kale with potatoes and cheese, binding them with egg yolk, bathing them in warm cream – now that's a lovely thing to do, and the result is a rich, warm, soul-satisfying dish, especially on a cold day.

Use thin-skinned potatoes, either red or white. Scrub them but leave the peeling on for texture. If you love the flavor of strong cheese, use Gruyère instead of the milder combination of Swiss and white Cheddar.

Serves 6 to 8

4	large red or white potatoes	4
1	medium onion, diced	1
4	slices back bacon, finely diced	
1 cup	Swiss cheese, shredded	250 mL
1 cup	white Cheddar, shredded	250 mL
1	bunch kale, shredded	1
	salt, pepper, nutmeg	
1	egg yolk	1
1 1/2 cups	half-and-half cream	375 mL

☐ Generously butter a shallow 8 cup (2L) casserole or gratin dish.

Thinly slice unpeeled potatoes, then cut into a coarse julienne. Place in a large bowl with the onion, diced bacon, half of each cheese, and the kale. Sprinkle with salt, pepper, and freshly grated nutmeg. Toss together to mix well and spoon into the casserole.

Put egg yolk in a small bowl and beat lightly. Heat half-and-half to scalding. Pour slowly into beaten egg yolk, whisking as you do. Pour over the potato-kale mixture. Sprinkle with remaining cheese. Bake, uncovered, in a 350 F (180 C) oven for about 1 hour, or until potatoes are very tender and the top forms a golden crust. Serve with roast chicken.

Kale Soup with Sausage, Lisbon Style

For this winter soup, use a coarse garlic sausage or other slow-smoked sausage, sliced about 1/2 inch (1.25 cm) thick. Traditionally, this soup has a spoonful of olive oil poured into it for flavor and heft, but I like it better if the toast is brushed with olive oil. This soup needs only a glass of ale or a simple red wine to finish it off.

Serves 4

1 cup	garlic sausage slices	250 mL
4 cups	beef or chicken broth	1 L
1	large yellow onion, diced	1
2	large potatoes, peeled and diced	2
1	bunch kale, thinly sliced	1
	salt and pepper to taste	
	toasted French bread or baguettes	
	garlic-infused olive oil	

☐ Cook sausage slices in a bit of water in a covered saucepan or in the microwave to render out some of the fat. Drain, cool, and coarsely chop the sausage.

Bring the broth to a boil. Add onion and potatoes, and simmer until tender. Mash with a potato masher. With a sharp knife, shred the kale fine, as though for coleslaw slaw. Add sausage and kale to the mixture in the pot, and simmer about 30 minutes – the soup will be thick. If you want a thinner soup, add enough skim milk to bring it to the desired texture. Add salt and pepper to taste.

Meanwhile, toast the French bread or baguette slices and brush them with garlic-infused olive oil. Put about 3 baguette slices in the bottom of each bowl and ladle the soup over them.

Chapter 20 ■ Kohlrabi

ONE OF THE FUNNIEST LOOKING PLANTS IN THE GARDEN, KOHLRABI LOOKS like a space vegetable, the sort of thing I'd expect to run across in a Martian garden. Neither a root nor a head, it's a swollen mainstem with leaves sprouting all the way around it on other stems.

Like kale, kohlrabi has always been more popular in central and northern Europe than in North America, and it's been on tables in the Far East for centuries. Happily, it's becoming a regular at farmers markets and major produce departments.

IN THE MARKET: The small, unscarred bulbs will be sweeter and firmer than big ones. Look for tennis-ball size or smaller. They're usually sold without the leaves, which is too bad as the entire plant is edible – leaves, stems, the whole kaboodle.

■ *Nutrition:* Contains calcium, potassium, and phosphorus. Has some vitamin C. Forty calories per cup (250 mL), raw.

■ *Season:* Local markets from early July through late September. Season is slightly longer for commercial varieties.

■ *Buy:* 1 small bulb per person; 2 if they're really small.

IN THE KITCHEN: Clip off stems and leaves and keep them in a separate plastic bag. Refrigerate for up to a week.

Small, freshly harvested kohlrabi is crisp and juicy with firm, white flesh and a flavor like mild turnip or cabbage heart. I like this vegetable raw, seasoned with salt and pepper. If very young, the skin is tender enough to eat, so no need to peel.

Kohlrabi can be substituted for radishes in salads or for turnips in cooked dishes. It's good simply cubed, boiled, mashed, and served with lashings of butter and a wisp of freshly grated nutmeg. The small ones are terrific for stuffing: parboil for 10 minutes, hollow out, and stuff with any meat or savory filling you wish. Finish the dish in the oven with a little cream or other sauce.

Gratin of Kohlrabi
with Ham
in Dill Cream

Gratin of Kohlrabi with Ham in Dill Cream

Swaddling kohlrabi with a rich, velvety, dill-scented cream sauce studded with nuggets of ham is one of the most luxurious and comforting things that can be done in the autumn kitchen. Use a Black Forest or other well-smoked ham, or any leftover bits you have kicking around the freezer from the last bone-in ham buffet. Diced bacon, either side or back bacon, is also excellent in this savory concoction.

Use the broad, slicer side of a hand-grater to cut the kohlrabi into thin chips, or use the slicer blade of a food processor. A few kohlrabi leaves chopped into this dish will add extra flavor and color, but if the leaves aren't on the bulb when you buy it, don't worry. They're optional.

Serves 4 to 6

3 lbs	kohlrabi	1.5 kg
	kohlrabi leaves, chopped (optional)	
1 tbsp	butter	15 mL
2	cloves garlic, pressed	2
8 oz	Black Forest ham, finely diced	125 mL
1/4 cup	fresh dill, minced	50 mL
2	eggs	2
1/2 cup	whipping cream	125 mL
1/2 cup	Swiss or Gruyère cheese, grated	125 mL
	salt and pepper	

☐ If kohlrabi bulbs are large, peel them. Slice or grate into broad, thin chips and put in a bowl. Cover with cold water while making the sauce. Shred leaves, if using, and reserve.

In a small frying pan, melt butter. Add garlic and ham, and cook briefly over medium heat. Stir in dill and kohlrabi leaves, if using. Remove from heat.

In a medium bowl, lightly beat eggs and cream. Stir in ham mixture and add cheese. Season with salt and pepper.

Drain kohlrabi and pat dry. Turn into a well-buttered 8 cup (2 L) gratin dish (any fairly flat casserole will be fine). Pour the sauce over it. Bake at 350 F (180 C) for about 40 minutes, or until kohlrabi is tender. If it threatens to dry out, add a little milk. Serve with any roasted meat.

Chapter 21 ■ *Leeks*

FROM THE BEGINNING OF RECORDED TIME, LEEKS HAVE BEEN IN somebody's garden, somewhere. Ancient Egyptians grew leeks. So did the Chinese and the people in the valley of the Tigris and Euphrates.

In Wales, the leek symbolizes the victory of good old King Cadwallader over the rampaging Saxons, who were miserable at best and had turned especially nasty in the year 640. For the Welsh, the leek is a charmed vegetable, and they remember it every year on St. David's Day with a bit of leek worn proudly in the buttonhole.

IN THE MARKET: Leeks are milder, gentler onions, and those with fresh, green tops are the ones to look for. Supermarket leeks occasionally have yellowed tops and tough, rootsy bases that are big and overgrown. They'll be stringy and strong-flavored. Avoid them.

The best leeks for the dish offered here are small, tender ones with fresh, white bottoms no more than 1 1/2 inches (3.75 cm) in diameter.

■ *Nutrition:* At roughly the same number of calories as onions (125 per large leek), they have trace amounts of several minerals and vitamins including vitamins C and A and some iron. A good source of fiber.

■ *Season:* Available year-round but peak October through May

■ *Buy:* If you're braising leeks, allow one per person.

IN THE KITCHEN: Leeks can be stored, unwashed, for about 1 week in plastic.

To prepare leeks for cooking, trim off root ends as they'll be hard and woody. Clip the tops, leaving 2 to 3 inches (5 to 7.5 cm) of green. Split lengthwise and wash under cool, running water to rid them of sand, which is the traditional growing medium.

Cold Leek Terrine, Bistro Style

Gratin of Leeks with Cream and Cheese

Leek and Yam Tart with Basil and Mozzarella

Cold Leek Terrine, Bistro Style

This is a common dish in bistros throughout France where it's often served as a first course with a simple balsamic or red wine vinaigrette. It's one of the most delicious dishes of that sort, with the delicately earthy flavor of young leeks in a cool beef aspic splashed with the sharper flavors of the shallot vinaigrette. It's a lovely appetizer to serve in spring or summer, although I've eaten it in November and enjoyed it thoroughly.

Use a terrine or loaf pan for this, either pyrex or enamel.

Serves 6 to 8

10 to 12	young, slender leeks	10 to 12
4	young, slender carrots	4
1	10 oz (284 mL) can beef consommé	1
1 tbsp	lemon juice	15 mL
1/2 tsp	black pepper	2 mL

Shallot Vinaigrette

Makes about 1 1/4 cups

3/4 cup	extra-virgin olive oil	175 mL
1/3 cup	red wine vinegar	75 mL
4 or 5	shallots, finely minced	4 or 5
1/4 cup	fresh parsley, minced	50 mL
	salt and pepper	

☐ Place all ingredients for vinaigrette in a small jar, cover tightly, and shake until emulsified. Reserve.

Trim and clean the leeks as indicated. Cook in barely simmering, salted water until tender. This will take roughly 12 minutes – they should not be overcooked but must be easily cut. Test with the tip of a paring knife after about 8 minutes.

Carefully drain the leeks, keeping them intact as much as possible and pressing gently to remove as much water as possible. Lift onto a thick kitchen towel and pat to absorb remaining moisture.

Meanwhile, peel carrots. Cook the carrots whole, in boiling water, until easily pierced with a knife. Carefully drain, taking care not to break them.

Line a terrine or loaf pan with parchment or waxed paper, sprayed with a non-stick coating. Lay the leeks in it in layers, with the root end facing one direction in the first layer and the opposite direction in the second layer. Use half the leeks.

Trim the carrots to fit, if necessary, and lay them on top of the leeks. Cover the carrots with the remaining leeks. Press down firmly, cover with waxed paper, and refrigerate until cold, about 3 hours.

Remove from refrigerator, pour in the undiluted beef consommé whisked with the lemon juice and pepper.

(Continued on page 130)

Cold Leek Terrine, Bistro Style

(Continued from page 129)

Return terrine to refrigerator. The consommé will jell in about three hours.

To serve, unmold the terrine on a small platter or oblong serving dish. Carefully remove the wax paper. Trim off any scraggly bits at the end and slice with a very sharp knife. Serve two slices per person, drizzled with the vinaigrette and accompanied by fresh hot toast.

Gratin of Leeks with Cream and Cheese

One of the great, simple dishes of northern France, this gratin was originally baked in an open hearth. Some restaurants in Normandy still do their gratins, tarts, and flatbreads this way, which likely explains why the last serving in the dish is often scorched.

Leaving aside the unquestioned rustic charm of the open hearth, your oven-baked gratin will be just as good, and nobody will get stuck with the burned bits.

Serves 6

2 lbs	young leeks	1 kg
2 tbsp	butter	30 mL
2 tbsp	flour	30 mL
1 cup	half-and-half cream	250 mL
1/2 cup	Swiss cheese, grated	125 mL
1/2 cup	Cheddar, grated	125 mL
1 cup	seasoned croutons, crushed	250 mL
	freshly ground pepper	

Clean leeks as directed. Poach in a little water until tender. Arrange in a buttered gratin dish.

To make sauce, melt butter over medium heat, stir in flour and cook, stirring, until all the butter has been absorbed and the mixture bubbles. With a wire whisk, gradually incorporate the cream. Continue stirring until sauce thickens.

Whisk in half the cheese. Pour over leeks in gratin dish. Top with remaining cheese and crouton crumbs. Bake, uncovered, in a 375 F (190 C) oven for 20 minutes, until lightly browned.

Leek and Yam Tart with Basil and Mozzarella

I first ate this delectable tart in a Westin Hotel, and the chef was kind enough to send me the recipe. As with most recipes, I couldn't leave well enough alone, and it has been adapted to fit my own quirks and personal taste.

It's important to use really young, tender leeks and fresh herbs here, both for the flavor and the aroma, which will be different depending on which variety of basil you use. I prefer the large, tender leaves of Genoa basil, but cinnamon basil works well, too, adding a subtle note of sweet spice.

Frozen phyllo dough is available in ethnic markets and most supermarkets. I use Krinos brand, which is sold by the pound and contains 20 rectangular sheets in a 16 oz (454 g) package. This recipe requires only 10 sheets, so the remaining dough can be wrapped in plastic and refrigerated for a few days to be used in something else.

Serves 6 to 8

1	medium yam, about 8 oz (250 g)	1
1 lb	young leeks	500 g
1	apple, peeled, finely diced	1
8 oz	mozzarella, grated	250 g
2	sprigs fresh thyme, minced	2
8 oz	phyllo pastry, thawed	250 g
1/4 cup	butter, melted	50 mL
8	large, fresh basil leaves (double amount if leaves are small)	8
	salt and freshly ground pepper	
	thyme for garnish	

☐ Peel the yam and slice it as thinly as possible. Put in a small saucepan, cover with water, and bring to a boil. Simmer about 5 minutes, until slightly softened. Drain.

Trim roots and tops of leeks, leaving about 1 inch (2.5 cm) of green. Slice leeks in half lengthwise and wash well under running water to remove any lingering sand. Slice leeks crosswise into 1 inch pieces (2.5 cm). Place in a bowl and cover with boiling water. Leave about 30 seconds to soften slightly. Drain well, pressing to remove water.

Toss the finely diced apple, grated mozzarella, and 2 sprigs of minced thyme together in a bowl.

Preheat oven to 325 F (160 C). Butter a 9 inch (1 L) pie plate.

Remove thawed phyllo pastry from the refrigerator. The key to success with phyllo is to keep it from drying out, so place the thawed phyllo on a damp towel and fold the towel over top so the dough remains moist. As you unroll each sheet, place it on a second damp towel, which will be your work surface. I find I can get

(Continued on page 132)

Leek and Yam Tart with Basil and Mozzarella

(Continued from page 131)

away with peeling four sheets at a time, but if I try to do more than that they start to tear.

Generously brush each sheet with melted butter and position in the baking dish, overlapping the sheets so the long overhanging ends of pastry are evenly distributed around the plate.

Layer in half the sliced yams, sprinkling lightly with salt and freshly ground pepper. Sprinkle some of the cheese mixture over the yam layer. Add a layer of leeks, using half of them, and half the basil leaves, distributing them evenly over the leeks. Add another layer of the cheese mixture.

Repeat the layers, ending with cheese.

Quickly fold the overlapping phyllo leaves over the tart. This will look higgeldy-piggeldy, which is part of its charm. Brush it with any remaining butter.

Bake 35 to 45 minutes, until pastry is a rich golden brown. Let the tart rest about 10 minutes before cutting with a sharp knife. Garnish with sprigs of fresh thyme.

Mushroom Variation: Add a layer of sliced, sautéed brown mushrooms or scatter a few soaked wild mushrooms, coarsely chopped, over the yams before adding the leeks. Fresh oyster mushrooms are also delicious in this dish.

Chapter 22 ■ *Lettuce*

ONCE THERE WAS ICEBERG LETTUCE. THEN THERE WAS ROMAINE. FOR A short season, there was leaf lettuce. And that pretty much did it for salads on this side of the Atlantic.

Even the old standby with the throwaway name – the tossed salad – was an orderly event. Iceberg, tomato, a few carrot curls. A cook who lived dangerously might rub the salad bowl with garlic before tossing, but that was about it for adventures in salad.

That's history. Enough of the boring stuff. At last the salad has come into its own. A mess of wild greens, clipped in the first flush of youth and tossed with a little good oil and vinegar and a wisp of salt – now that's a salad. In the garden it's known as mesclun, meaning cut and come again.

In early spring, a mixture of seeds (leaf lettuce, sorrel, spinach, cress, mache, basil, chicory, dandelion, arugula) is broadcast over a carefully prepared seed bed where as many rogue weeds as possible have been turfed out. This is important because of the harvest method – a general scything of the crowded little plants with a paring knife or shears.

A few weeks after planting, there's your salad, ready for snipping. It will be a bit of everything: frilly, ferny, scalloped, mild, peppery.

Seed houses now carry pre-mixed salad seeds, and you can order the variety you like, from the mild northern Italian mixtures to the zingier ones labeled Nicoise. Some seed houses are more creative than others and will custom blend for you: warm or cool plants, bitter or sweet plants, early, mid-season, or late. One of the joys of mesclun plots is that you can grow several different kinds in a summer, harvesting them as the season progresses.

Mesclun Salad with Goat Cheese Croutons

Not Exactly Caesar Salad

from The Garden

In my own garden, which gets less sun than I'd like for other plants, I've had great success with mesclun. Picking a salad involves an ever-changing palate of aromas, colors, and textures, from the first leaves of pale green or red ruffled lettuces to blue-green feathers of young dill and the burgundy tones of opal basil.

If you don't have a garden, the market will have a variety of greens and herbs. Buy the smallest possible amounts in the greatest variety, and as soon as they've been washed and dried, toss them with the vinaigrette of your choice. I like a fairly sharp one with lemon juice and garlic in extra-virgin olive oil, but this is a good time to experiment with other oils: walnut or hazelnut if you have some, or one of your home-infused oils. They complement the nippier greens.

■ Frozen Vietnamese spring rolls, brushed with oil and baked in a hot oven, are delicious wrapped in leaf lettuce. Serve a napkin-lined basket of hot spring rolls, another basket of mixed lettuce leaves, and accompany them with a spicy dip or plum sauce sharpened with vinegar. Soft lettuces such as red leaf, butter, or Grand Rapids leaf work best here.

■ Serve small, crisp, inside leaves of romaine, endive, or iceberg lettuce as scoops to hold small servings of couscous salad, shrimp salad, chicken salad. Arrange a variety of them on a serving tray. Or serve several leaves with individual bread bowls of spicy chili. (Hollow out crusty Italian rolls, brush with melted butter, and bake briefly before ladling in the chili.)

■ Shred romaine, arugula, or radicchio. Toss with garlic-infused oil, then toss everything with hot vermicelli. Finish with crumbled bacon and grated Parmesan cheese.

Mesclun Salad with Goat Cheese Croutons

Spring varieties of mesclun have the greenest, gentlest flavors of the entire season, and pairing them with the young, mildly acidic goat cheese on warm croutons makes an inspired dish.

Don't let an overenthusiastic cheese monger talk you into an older cheese for the spring mesclun as old goat cheese becomes distinctly goaty, both in aroma and flavor, and would overwhelm the delicacy of the baby greens. Later in the season, when the mesclun variety changes and the flavors are somewhat sassier, try combining the goat cheese with some mashed feta or (for an entirely different taste) grated, aged Cheddar.

Serves 4

4	large handfuls of mixed young lettuces	4
	handful of spinach leaves	
1 cup	loose-packed basil leaves	250 mL
	snipping herbs: parsley, chives, oregano, sorrel	

(Continued on page 136)

Mesclun Salad with Goat Cheese Croutons

(Continued from page 135)

Vinaigrette for Salad Greens

1/2 cup	extra-virgin olive oil	125 mL
1/4 cup	red wine vinegar	50 mL
	juice of 1 lemon	
1/2 tsp	sugar	2 mL
1/2 tsp	dry mustard	2 mL
1	clove garlic, pressed	1
	salt and pepper	

Croutons

8	thin baguette slices, toasted	8
8 oz	snow goat cheese, mashed	250 mL
1 tbsp	soft butter	15 mL
	black pepper, coarsely ground	

☐ Wash the greens, pat or spin dry, and pile into a large bowl. The leaves will be naturally small, but any larger ones can be torn. Snip or tear herbs of your choice over them.

Place vinaigrette ingredients in a jar and shake vigorously. Reserve.

Stir soft butter and mashed cheese together. Moments before serving, spread cheese on toasted baguette slices, sprinkle with coarsely ground black pepper, and run under broiler just until cheese begins to bubble.

Drizzle vinaigrette over greens mixture and toss quickly, adding salt judiciously, grinding pepper over it at the last second. Pile onto salad plates and top with hot goat cheese croutons.

Feta Variation: If you can't find fresh snow goat cheese, use a mild feta instead, or even camemzola mashed with a few toasted walnuts.

Not Exactly Caesar Salad

The Caesar salad has become such a classic that any variation is taken in some quarters as a personal insult.

Phooey. Where would civilization be if we had never changed anything? In a cave, that's where.

Here, then, is a variation on the Caesar theme. Instead of tearing the romaine, shred and combine with the softer leaves of butter lettuce. Instead of leaving fishy bits of anchovy cluttering up the bowl, combine buttery anchovy paste in a smoother, subtler blend with the oil and lemon. Different textures, familiar flavors, a terrific salad.

Serves 4

Croutons

	vegetable oil and a garlic clove	
6	slices French bread, cubed	6

Dressing

3/4 cup	olive oil	175 mL
1/4 cup	lemon juice	50 mL
1 tsp	anchovy paste	5 mL
2	cloves garlic, pressed	2
1 tsp	capers	5 mL
1/4 cup	freshly grated Parmesan	50 mL
	black pepper	

(Continued on page 138)

Not Exactly Caesar Salad

(Continued from page 137)

Salad and Toppings

1	head butter lettuce, torn	1
1	small head romaine, shredded	1
2 or 3	slices bacon, fried crisp and crumbled	2 or 3
	extra Parmesan cheese	

□ Heat oven to 325 F (160 C). Coat a cookie sheet with oil and rub well with a cut clove of garlic.

Trim crusts from bread and cut into generous cubes. Put cubes on the cookie sheet and oven-toast until light, golden brown, turning often. Turn the oven off and leave the cubes in the oven for about 30 minutes to crisp.

In a large salad bowl, beat oil, lemon juice, anchovy paste, garlic, capers, Parmesan, and a hefty grinding of black pepper. A fork or whisk works well for this chore.

Tear butter lettuce into the bowl over the vinaigrette and add shredded romaine. Crumble bacon over the top and sprinkle with croutons. Grate a little Parmesan cheese over the top, adjusting the amount to suit your taste.

Toss the salad and serve immediately.

Seafood Variation: Add 1 cup (250 mL) each cooked crab meat and cooked, cleaned shrimp meat to the salad just before tossing it. This becomes a meal-sized salad for four or an appetizer for six.

Chapter 23 ■ Mushrooms

IN MY PARTICULAR PATCH OF PRAIRIE, MUSHROOMS CAME IN A TIN CAN with a classy black label and the words *China Lily* written in gold script.

Though wild mushrooms were available for the picking, my family didn't eat them. Only the Ukrainian women knew which trees sheltered the pidpanki, which pastures had *stepovas,* and exactly how to dry, freeze, or can either one of them for future use. By some combination of instinct and luck, they avoided the deadly *Amanita virosa,* also known as the destroying angel.

But my mother was in all things a careful woman, and it wasn't in her to trust a toadstool. As far as she was concerned, wild mushrooms equaled toadstools, which equaled trouble: warts, rashes, stomach aches, and painful, lingering death. Not knowing the edibles from the incdibles, we confined ourselves to the tinny ones in the black can.

Years later, I landed on the other end of the gastronomic see-saw with the classiest relative of all mushrooms – the truffle.

Here's a mushroom that doesn't even bother to surface, but hides silently, underground, somewhere in some stony French field or lonely Italian woodland, waiting for the gently snuffling nose of the trained dog or pig that will unearth it.

Note the term *somewhere.* The exact location of truffle grounds are more closely guarded than the Pope's private number, and the hunting and marketing of truffles is riddled with secrets and ancient curses. It is carried on by smugglers, sneaks, and outrageous liars who love to brag about their skullduggery later on over a glass of something bracing in the local bar.

I have never truffled in France, though I hope to while I'm still up and walking. But I came close in Italy, home of the rare, white truffle.

Mushrooms with Green Herbs and Radishes

Mushroom Terrine Wrapped in Greens

Ragout of Wild Mushrooms in Shallot Cream

Oyster Mushrooms and Eggs in Sourdough Loaf

from The Garden

I'd been promised that I could accompany a hunter and his trusty dog, Bella, on one of their middle-of-the-night forays. Bella, a Heinz 57 mutt, was worth $5000 on the truffle circuit, thanks to her talented nose. She was famous for catching the musty, peppery, ethereal whiff of white truffle under the most adverse conditions, and her name was loudly praised in bars from Alba to Gubbio. I had a private chat with Bella and gave her half my ham sandwich to cement our friendship.

But the night before our foray, the hunter's grandmother stepped in. Only three types of female were allowed to go a-truffling: dogs, pigs, and virgins over 90 (of which, she assured me with a cackle, there were none in the village). I was, of course, disqualified. I'd distract Bella, bring bad luck, etc., though I figured luck had less to do with it than economics. Bella had once sniffed out a grapefruit-sized truffle that fetched a tidy $1400, and they didn't want some foreign woman blabbing about the location.

Snuffling about those woods that night, Bella and the hunters returned with a modest pile of seven large white truffles, just over two pounds. At about $55 an ounce, they'd make a cool $1650 tax-free.

Once the truffles were in the restaurants, they'd be carried to the table for weighing, then shaved reverently into the dish – a steaming ravioli stuffed with mild goat cheese and sage, or a baked potato splashed with grappa, or (best of the lot) a champagne risotto with wild berries, a wisp of Parmesan, and then – the truffles.

After dinner, the remaining bit of truffle would be weighed again. The customer would fork over a surcharge of about $80 per ounce of consumed truffle and go home content in the knowledge that nobody, not even the Pope, had dined so well that night.

Even without truffles (and most of us will be without), there are many hundreds of varieties of edible mushrooms, and to delve into them extensively we'd need a separate volume.

For our purposes in this book, fresh mushrooms can be divided into two camps: cultivated domestic and cultivated exotic.

IN THE MARKET: Here's a refreshing thought – the most expensive mushrooms are those that cost the most to grow. Simple logic. Consequently, two common domestic mushrooms, the white button and the Italian brown, are often the best buy. Both are firm, juicy, with a mild flavor and crisp texture.

Oyster mushrooms are a soft grey or creamy color, slightly frilled, with tender, fragile flesh, and a delicate, nutty flavor. They have a lower water content than buttons so won't weep as much during cooking. Now that they're being cultivated and grown on sterilized straw pillows, they're a lot easier to find in local markets.

Shitake mushrooms, also known as black Chinese mushrooms, have a nut-brown cap and

dense ivory flesh. Their strong, earthy flavor is sometimes described as smoky or woodsy.

Golden chanterelles are usually available dry, as are morels and porcini. The highly flavored porcini is a great favorite among Italian cooks and packs a lot of flavor. The chanterelle has a milder flavor and texture, and is lovely in sauces and omelets.

Enoki mushrooms have long, graceful stems and tiny, white caps, and in their infancy they resemble bean sprouts. So delicate is their flavor and texture that I use them as a raw garnish, even in hot dishes.

- **Nutrition:** Mushrooms are low in calories, only 20 per cup (250 mL), sliced, raw, and they contain a fair amount of potassium.

- **Season:** Year-round.

- **Buy:** About 4 oz (115 g) per person should do it.

IN THE KITCHEN:

- **Fresh mushrooms:** Store fresh mushrooms for as short a time as possible, but no longer than 4 days, in a closed paper bag. Do not store in plastic as they'll quickly deteriorate into a slimy sludge. Washing mushrooms is tricky as they absorb water quickly. Either wipe them with a damp towel or brush with a soft mushroom brush.

- **Dry mushrooms:** The intense, woodsy flavors of freshly picked, wild mushrooms are only available to those who know them well. For the rest of us, eating any mushroom we've picked in the wild is playing with fire. If you're charmed by the idea of mushrooming, take a course. Good ones are available in all major cities.

Meanwhile, there are dried mushrooms picked by knowledgeable mycologists. Dehydrated, they carry in their tiny, shriveled bodies an enormous amount of highly concentrated flavor. Although they're expensive, a little goes a long way, and when used with fresh mushrooms, they add depth and richness to the dish.

Look for dried mushrooms in gourmet shops, ethnic food shops, and farmers markets. Most of them come in little cellophane packages, so before you hand over such an investment, check to see that they haven't been mashed into a lot of bits and crumbs.

I find that dried mushrooms vary considerably among brands, no doubt due to harvest conditions and handling. The soaking time required to reconstitute them will therefore vary from 20 or 30 minutes to as long as an hour, depending on size, variety, and brand.

Cover the mushrooms with warm water, unless the directions specify hot, and check after 20 minutes. Common sense will tell you that when the mushrooms are pliable, they are ready to use. Strain them through a coffee filter and reserve the flavorful juices. Give the mushrooms one more quick rinse if they seem sandy, and proceed with your recipe.

Mushrooms with Green Herbs and Radishes

In this salad, the dark, roasted flavor of black rice vinegar with a great bash of freshly chopped herbs brings out the best in firm, white mushrooms and crisp radishes. Use either red radishes or thinly sliced daikon. If using daikon, look for a small one rather than the fibrous monsters that often show up in the markets. Both the flavor and the texture will be better.

Serves 8

2 lb	firm white mushrooms	1 kg
1	bunch large red radishes	1
	or	
1	medium daikon, sliced	1
1/4 cup	soy sauce	50 mL
1/3 cup	rice vinegar	75 mL
1/2 cup	canola oil	125 mL
1 tsp ea	sugar and salt	5 mL ea
1/2 cup	fresh parsley, chopped	125 mL
1/4 cup	cilantro, chopped	50 mL
1	green onion, minced	1
2 tsp	freshly grated ginger	10 mL
1	clove garlic, pressed	1

☐ If mushrooms are button-size, they may be brushed and left whole. Large mushrooms can be sliced or halved.

Slice mushrooms and radishes into a large plastic or glass container with a lid. Combine all remaining ingredients, whisk together, and pour over mushrooms and radishes. Refrigerate at least 2 hours, turning once or twice. Serve with buttered rye bread.

from The Garden

Ragout of Wild Mushrooms in Shallot Cream

This is an utterly delicious dish to serve for lunch or brunch, relying on the intense flavor of dried, wild mushrooms to give the dish strength.

If you can't find fresh oyster mushrooms in the market, try to find brown Italian ones. The flavor will vary slightly and the texture will be different, but it will still be a delectable dish.

Some cooks would make this sauce a pure reduction of cream and chicken stock, but there's so much flavor in the mushroom juices that I use a modified roux, browning a small amount of flour in the buttery juices left in the pan after the mushrooms have cooked.

For the puff pastry cases, use purchased pastry. It can be baked the day before. The sauce can be made ahead of time and kept warm in a double boiler or *bain marie.*

Salmon Variation: If you happen to have some nice red spring salmon sitting in your refrigerator, it could be quickly poached or microwaved, then sliced and folded into this. One salmon steak will be enough for 4.

Asparagus Variation: Tuck three or four short spears of lightly steamed asparagus in each pastry case before adding the mushrooms and sauce. Omit raw mushroom garnish.

Serves 6

6	puff pastry cases, baked as directed	6
1 cup	sliced oyster mushrooms	250 mL
2	small pkgs dried morels or porcini	2
2 cups	firm, white mushrooms	250 mL
1 tsp	oil	5 mL
2 tbsp	butter	30 mL
4	shallots, sliced	4
1 tbsp	flour	15 mL
2 cups	chicken stock	500 mL
2 tbsp	sour cream or crème fraîche	30 mL
1 tbsp	chopped dillweed, garnish	15 mL
6	slices of raw white mushroom, garnish	6

☐ When pastry cases are baked, remove the lids and reserve them. Pull some of the center out of the pastry cases to create a small cup.

Buy 2 packages (3/8 oz / 10 g) of dried mushrooms. Reconstitute the mushrooms by covering with warm water until soft and pliable (20 to 30 minutes). Strain through a coffee filter, pressing the mushrooms well to extract every bit of the flavorful juice. Reserve the liquid. If a lot of sand appears in the filter, quickly rinse the mushrooms again. Squeeze them to remove excess water.

Coarsely chop the reconstituted mushrooms.

Cut fresh mushrooms into quarters.

Wipe a large frying pan with 1 tsp (5 mL) oil and melt the butter in it.

Starting with the white ones, stir-fry mushrooms until they begin to brown. Remove with a slotted spoon to a bowl. Add the oyster mushrooms and finally the morels or porcini, turning them quickly in the juices. Remove with a slotted spoon, adding them to the other mushrooms.

Put the shallots in the pan and stir them, cooking about 3 minutes. Add the strained liquid from the dried mushrooms. Increase the heat and cook it down to about 1/2 cup (125 mL).

Sprinkle flour into the pan and stir until it browns. There will be very little roux, but you don't need much. Whisk in chicken stock. When the sauce comes to a simmer, correct the seasoning with salt and pepper. If the sauce is very thin, continue cooking until it is reduced by about one-third.

Whisk in the sour cream or crème fraîche and dill. Taste for seasoning. Fold in the mushrooms.

On individual plates, spoon the mushrooms into the pastry cases, letting the sauce overflow generously. Garnish the top with a wisp of dill and a slice of raw mushroom. Replace the lid of the pastry case, propped at a rakish angle.

Oyster Mushrooms and Eggs in Sourdough Loaf

Find a good baker whose sourdough has a coarse texture and a magnificent crust so you can hollow it out. Brushed with butter and filled with mushrooms and softly scrambled eggs, this makes a lovely brunch dish.

If you can't find oyster mushrooms, substitute either fresh brown Italian mushrooms or a package of dried porcini or morels, prepared according to package directions.

Serves 4

1	round sourdough loaf	1
1/4 cup	soft butter	50 mL
2	slices bacon, diced	2
1 tbsp	butter	15 mL
1	small sweet pepper, sliced	1
12	oyster mushrooms, quartered	12
2 cups	white mushrooms, sliced	500 mL
10	eggs, lightly beaten	10
	salt and pepper	
1/4 cup	Cheddar cheese, grated	50 mL

☐ Preheat oven to 325 F (160 C).

With a bread knife, carefully remove the top 1/3 of the loaf. Reserve lid. Pull the soft interior out of the crust, reserving it for another use. Leave a shell about 1/2 inch (1.25 cm) thick.

Using a pastry brush, generously coat inside of the loaf with soft butter. Place on a cookie sheet and bake for about 10 minutes, just long enough to lightly toast the inside of the loaf.

Dice the bacon. Put it in a large frying pan with 1 tbsp (15 mL) butter and fry until nearly crisp. Add sweet peppers, oyster mushrooms, and white mushrooms. Cook until mushrooms have given up their juices, then turn up the heat to reduce the juice and soften the peppers. If it seems dry, add a little more butter to the pan.

Season the lightly beaten eggs with salt and pepper, and pour into the pan with the bacon and vegetables. Cook, stirring, over low heat until softly scrambled.

Pile into the toasted loaf, strew the top with grated Cheddar, and return to the oven just until the eggs are set and the cheese melted. Serve in wedges with more bacon and wild berry preserves.

Chapter 24 ▪ Onions

I COULD NO MORE RUN A KITCHEN WITHOUT ONIONS THAN I COULD without garlic. It's unthinkable.

After centuries of playing Cinderella to the rest of the produce world, these lilies of the kitchen are finally getting some respect. Give thanks.

The single fault of the onion is its sulfuric properties, which leave a lingering odor and bring on floods of painful tears. Cutting into an onion allows minute amounts of volatile sulfur to dissolve in the natural moisture in our eyes. It produces a dilute form of sulfuric acid; thus the tears.

IN THE MARKET: There are many onions on the market, from tiny pearl onions to small and potent boilers to the reliable yellow and white cooking onions and the sweetly mild Maui, Vidalia, and Walla Wallas. Two Italian red onions are also worth finding: the mild torpedo and the hotter flat red. Beyond that we have the relatives: garlic, shallots, leeks, green onions or scallions, and chives.

Shallots and garlic grow in the same pattern – a head of smaller cloves within the outer papery skin. However, shallots are delicately flavored and extremely tender.

Each member of the onion group is wonderful in its own way. They are the power behind a great clutch of good cooking: soups, breads, and sauces.

▪ *Nutrition:* One green onion contains less than 5 calories and a fair amount of vitamin A. Dry-skinned onions contain vitamin C, and one cup (250 mL), cooked, has only 36 calories. Shallots are high in iron.

▪ *Season:* Year-round for most onions, with sweet varieties such as Vidalia, Maui, and Walla Walla easier to find in late summer. Sweet onions have delicate flesh and a shorter storage life than the hard, dry-skinned keepers.

Three Onion Soup

Sweet Onion Confit with Raisins

Green Onion Crepes

Baked Onion Slices Parmigiana

Red Onion Salad with Honey Mustard Sauce

Buttery Stuffed Onions

Embered Pearl Onions

Baby Onions in Mustard Cream

from The Garden

■ **_Buy:_** For boilers, count on two or three per person. Buy one medium onion per person if you're baking them.

IN THE KITCHEN: Green onions should be refrigerated, unwashed, in plastic, for 5 to 7 days. Shallots, garlic, and dry-skinned onions should be stored in a cool, dark, dry place that is well-ventilated. They'll keep this way for several weeks. Don't try to store them in plastic.

How to peel onions without tears? Some cooks hold their breath! Others swear by refrigerating the onion first, supposedly to stabilize the volatile oils that make us weep. Others leave the root-end on during peeling. And so forth. For me, nothing works. Pass the Kleenex.

For how to peel pearl or baby onions, see note immediately before the recipes.

When preparing onions for boiling or braising, cut a shallow x in the root end to keep the layers from billowing off.

Three Onion Soup

Nothing is as welcoming on a cold evening as a bowl of onion soup. By combining several onions in the same soup, we gather the best qualities of this favorite vegetable family into one steaming, aromatic pot and then bake it with cheese-covered croutons that have been lightly kissed with garlic.

Serves 6

3	large yellow onions	3
3	red onions	3
1 tbsp	oil	15 mL
3	cloves garlic, pressed	3
1	basket of pearl onions	1
1 tbsp	flour	15 mL
8 cups	beef or chicken broth	2 L
1 cup	dry white wine	250 mL
	salt and pepper	
6	French bread croutons	6
1	clove garlic	1
1 1/2 cups	mixed cheese, shredded	375 mL

☐ Slice yellow and red onions, and place in a large pot or Dutch oven with the oil. Cover and cook 10 minutes over medium heat to sweat the onions. Uncover, add garlic and peeled pearl onions, and continue cooking, stirring frequently, until golden brown.

Sprinkle with flour and stir until the flour seems to melt into the onion. At this point, stir in beef broth and wine, and add salt and pepper. Cover and simmer on lowest heat for about 45 minutes.

Brush toasted French bread with garlic-infused olive oil or rub the crouton with a cut clove of garlic. Taste soup to correct seasonings and ladle into individual oven-proof bowls. Top with a crouton and sprinkle generously with cheese – a mixture of mozzarella and Swiss works very well. Place bowls in a 400 F (200 C) oven and bake until cheese bubbles. Some people have been known to splash a little port into their bowl just as it comes from the oven, but that's really gilding the lily.

Sweet Onion Confit with Raisins

The imposing flavor of large, yellow onions is greatly enhanced by slow stewing with sugar, spices, and big, juicy raisins. Slice onions in a food processor to avoid shedding a bucket of tears.

This is a wonderful sauce to serve with grilled chicken or pork tenderloin and rice, couscous, or creamy mashed potatoes. It also makes a delicious topping for pizza.

Makes about 3 cups (750 mL)

1 tbsp	olive oil	15 mL
2 tbsp	butter	30 mL
6	large onions, peeled and sliced lengthwise	6
1/2 tsp ea	salt, ginger, cloves, thyme	2 mL ea
1 tsp ea	curry powder and cinnamon	5 mL ea
1 tsp	yellow mustard seed	5 mL
3 tbsp	brown sugar	45 mL
2 cups	chicken stock	500 mL
1 cup	golden raisins	250 mL
1/2	lemon, unpeeled, sliced paper thin	1/2

☐ In a Dutch oven, melt butter in olive oil. Add onions, cooking and stirring over medium heat until transparent (don't let them brown). Sprinkle with salt, spices, and sugar. Cover and cook over low heat for about 20 minutes. Uncover, add chicken stock, raisins, and lemon, and continue cooking at a simmer until the juice is reduced and the sauce has thickened.

This sauce can be stored in the refrigerator for several days and reheated when needed.

Green Onion Crepes

Unlike the greasy, leaden, green onion pancakes that have become almost endemic in Chinese restaurants, these onion crepes have a delicate texture and a real thump of flavor from the onions, garlic, chilies, and oriental sauces.

Use the crepes as an accompaniment to barbecued duck or almost any barbecued meat: lamb, pork, chicken. These are also wonderful with a stir-fry of chicken, lamb, or pork, and can be used as wrappers for *mu-shu* pork or even salad.

Makes about 1 dozen

1 tbsp ea	sesame oil and canola oil	15 mL ea
12	green onions, diced	12
1 cup	flour	250 mL
4	large eggs, beaten	4
1 cup	beer or soda water, room temperature	250 mL
2 tbsp ea	rice vinegar and soy sauce	30 mL ea
2	cloves garlic, pressed	2
2	small, dried, red chilies, crushed	2
1 1/2 tsp	salt	7 mL

☐ In a large frying pan, heat both oils. Add onions. Stir-fry about 30 seconds, then turn off the burner.

In a medium bowl, mix flour, eggs, and beer or soda water. Add all remaining ingredients and beat with a wire whisk until fairly smooth. Add onions with their juices. Let batter rest 15 minutes in refrigerator. Batter should be the consistency of thick cream. If it's too thick, add a little more beer.

Coat a 6 inch (15 cm) crepe pan with oil or a non-stick spray. Heat. Ladle about 1/4 cup (50 mL) into the hot pan and swirl to distribute batter. When edges turn brown, flip the pancake and cook other side. Lay pancakes on a paper towel-lined tray and keep warm. Make remaining pancakes.

To serve, fold in quarters and arrange on a platter. Tuck wisps of cilantro or green onion in here and there. Offer Firecracker Sauce and a platter of thinly sliced barbecued duck, including the crisp skin.

(Continued on page 154)

from The Garden

Green Onion Crepes

(Continued from page 153)

Firecracker Sauce

Makes 2 cups (500 mL)

1 cup	Chinese plum sauce	250 mL
2	cloves garlic, pressed	2
1/2 cup	black rice vinegar	125 mL
2 tbsp	soy sauce	30 mL
2 tsp	freshly grated ginger	10 mL
2 tsp	dried chilies, crushed	10 mL
1/4 cup	water	50 mL
	green onion tops, minced	

☐ In a small saucepan, combine all ingredients except onion tops. Bring to a boil. Reduce heat and simmer 10 minutes. Pour into a blender and process until nearly smooth. Cool slightly and stir in minced onion top.

Baked Onion Slices Parmigiana

Use new-crop sweet onions, possibly Walla-Walla, Vidalia, Maui, or Italian red for this easy dish. The mayonnaise seals in the juices and bakes the onions just enough to soften them and bring out all their natural sweetness. These are fantastic with steak.

Serves 6

3	large onions	3
1/2 cup	mayonnaise	125 mL
1/2 cup	dry bread crumbs	125 mL
1/2 cup	freshly grated Parmesan or Asiago cheese	125 mL

☐ Slice onions 1/2 inch (1.25 cm) thick. With a pastry brush, coat both sides of onion slices with mayonnaise. In a small dish, stir together dry bread crumbs and Parmesan cheese. Carefully dredge onion slices in cheese and crumb mixture, keeping each slice together if possible.

Lay slices on a cookie sheet sprayed with a non-stick cooking spray. Bake in a 400 F (200 C) oven until golden, about 15 minutes. Using a spatula, turn the slices and continue baking about 10 minutes. Remove carefully with a spatula and serve with any grilled meat.

Onions Baked in Their Skins

Like beets and potatoes, onions roasted in their skins develop sweetness and their flavor intensifies. Meanwhile, with all its juices captured inside as it bakes, the onion becomes meltingly soft. In the market, look for Walla Walla sweets or any good-sized, sweet onion from the new crop.

The oven temperature isn't terribly important. They can bake along with whatever else is in the oven for dinner. When they're squeezable and easily pierced, they're done.

To serve, cut the onion in half and add butter, salt, and pepper.

Red Onion Salad with Honey Mustard Sauce

This salad is perfect with barbecued pork steak, veal steak, or grilled chicken.

The sweet mustard sauce is adapted from my late Aunt Roma. Such was the reputation of Roma's mustard-spiked double boiler dressing that no member of my father's family has ever attempted a potato salad without a batch of it standing by. Probably they never will.

My version makes a smashing sauce for blanched red onions, which become slightly soft while retaining their crunch. Served with steak and baked potatoes, it's unbeatable.

Serves 8

3	large red onions, thinly sliced	3
1/2 cup	fresh chives, minced	125 mL
1/4 cup	fresh parsley, minced	50 mL

Honey Mustard Sauce

1 tsp	salt	5 mL
2 tsp	dry mustard	10 mL
2 tbsp	flour	30 mL
1/4 cup	honey	50 mL
2	eggs	2
1 cup	water	250 mL
1/2 cup	vinegar	125 mL

☐ Place sliced onions in a colander and pour boiling water over them. Drain and refresh under cold water. Place in a glass bowl with chives and parsley. Drizzle with sweet mustard sauce and toss gently.

To make sauce, combine dry ingredients in top half of a double boiler. Beat together the honey, eggs, water, and vinegar, and beat into dry mixture. Cook over boiling water, beating with an electric mixer at lowest setting until mixture thickens to the consistency of thick cream. Cool.

Buttery Stuffed Onions

Almost any herb butter could be used in this easy onion dish, but it is essentially a fall dish to be served with roasts or game birds, so it takes especially well to sage and thyme.

Serves 4

1/4 cup	butter	50 mL
1/2 cup	feta cheese, crumbled	125 mL
1/2 cup	Cheddar cheese, grated	125 mL
1 cup	fresh bread crumbs	250 mL
1/4 tsp ea	sage and thyme	1 mL ea
4	medium yellow onions	4
4	fresh or dried sage leaves	4

☐ Mix together butter, cheeses, bread crumbs, sage, and dried thyme.

Peel onions. Cut into five segments from top almost to the root. Separate slightly and stuff with butter-cheese mixture. Lay a sage leaf on each one. Place in a buttered casserole just big enough to hold the onions snugly. Cover and bake at 350 F (180 C) about 25 minutes, or until tender, adding a little water if the onions threaten to dry out.

Uncover and bake 10 minutes longer, basting with juices. Serve hot.

Embered Pearl Onions

Pearl onions, sometimes marketed as silver skin onions, or Barlettas if you have a dedicated grower, are fiddley to prepare, but this is such an excellent side dish for autumn that it's worth the crying and the peeling. To make the job easier, slice top and bottom off each little onion and when you have about 4 cups (1 L) of onions, pour boiling water over them and leave for about 5 minutes. They'll peel easily, and you won't have to shed further tears. The initial caramelizing starts the flavor on its way, but finishing the dish under the broiler (or over the coals) is what brings out the final drop of sweetness, perfectly matched by the aromatic vinegar.

Serve these hot or cold, as part of an antipasto, or as a delectable garnish with game birds or roasts.

Serves 8

1 tbsp	butter	15 mL
1 tbsp	oil	15 mL
4 cups	pearl onions, peeled	1 L
	salt and pepper	
1 tbsp	granulated sugar	15 mL
3 tbsp	balsamic or Chinkiang vinegar	45 mL

☐ Melt butter and oil in a large frying pan. Add pearl onions. Season lightly, sprinkle with sugar, and shake the pan back and forth so the onions are well coated. Cover and let onions cook in their own juices for about 10 minutes, watching carefully. The moment they begin to caramelize, drizzle with the vinegar.

Now place the pan in the oven about 4 inches (10 cm) from the broiler and let the onions glaze and brown, shaking the pan occasionally.

Baby Onions in Mustard Cream

Baby onions, also known as boilers, are a size larger than pearl but should be not bigger than a golf ball. Buy three per person, with a couple of extras, for this traditional Thanksgiving favorite.

Serves 8

28	small boiling onions	28
3 tbsp	butter	45 mL
3 tbsp	flour	45 mL
1 1/2 cups	hot milk	375 mL
1 tbsp	Dijon mustard	15 mL
1/2 tsp	salt	2 mL

☐ Cut top and root ends off onions and put onions in a large bowl. Pour boiling water over them and let stand 5 minutes for easier, tear-free peeling. Drain, peel, and cut a shallow X in the root end to keep the layers from separating.

Put onions in a medium saucepan, cover with water, and bring to a boil. Cook onions until just tender, about 20 minutes. Drain and hold until ready for the sauce. (This step can be done a day ahead. Refrigerate.)

To make the sauce, melt butter in a medium saucepan. Add flour and cook, stirring until butter is absorbed into the flour paste; be careful it doesn't brown. Remove from heat. Beat in milk, mustard, and salt with a wire whisk.

Put drained onions in an 8 cup (2 L) casserole. Pour mustard cream over top and bake in a 325 F (160 C) oven until bubbly.

Chapter 25 ■ Parsnips

Sugar-Glazed
Parsnips

PERSONALLY, I COULD LIVE WITHOUT PARSNIPS. TART THEM UP WITH butter and sugar and other fiddley cosmetics if you will, they still taste like parsnips to me.

A few weeks ago, I listened to an eminent dietitian lecture about the virtues of vegetables. When she got to parsnips she went on about their vitamins, their laudable potassium content, their fiber, their handy carbohydrate content. Then she dropped a bomb – parsnips contain trace amounts of a subtle poison known as furocoumarin.

True, you'd have to feed your average laboratory rat about a ton of them before he'd show any ill effects, but I pricked up my ears, applauded loudly, and felt vindicated for ignoring parsnips whenever possible. Still, I'm a broad-minded cook, and if you must have 'em, I've found a pretty good way to do them up.

IN THE MARKET: Look for small parsnips, which will be sweeter and less inclined to be woody. Be sure they have no bruises or mold.

■ *Nutrition:* Good source of fiber; high in vitamin A and potassium. About 100 calories per cup (250 mL), diced.

■ *Season:* November through March. A good frost sweetens them, turning the starch to sugar and producing a rather nutty flavor.

■ *Buy:* One parsnip per person should be enough.

IN THE KITCHEN: Store parsnips, unwashed, in a plastic bag in the refrigerator, for a week. To cook, trim tops and root ends. Peel and wash.

Sugar-Glazed Parsnips

These are the only excuse I can find for buying parsnips.

Serves 4

4	medium parsnips	4
4 tbsp	butter	60 mL
2 tbsp	brown sugar	30 mL
	juice of 1 lemon	
	salt and pepper	

☐ Peel parsnips and slice lengthwise into 3 or 4 slices each.

Place in a saucepan and cover with water. Bring to a boil and cook until barely fork-tender. Drain and reserve.

Melt butter in a large frying pan. Add parsnips and fry until lightly browned. Sprinkle with sugar. Turn, fry on the other side, and sprinkle with lemon juice. Turn heat as low as possible and continue cooking until parsnips are well glazed and tender. Add a little water if necessary to keep them juicy.

Spoon into a serving dish and pour the pan juices over them. (There won't be a lot of juice, but you should scrape out every bit.) Serve hot. Salt and pepper to taste.

Chapter 26 ▪ Peas

THERE ARE FEW THINGS SWEETER THAN STANDING IN YOUR OWN garden, up to your knees in pea vines, with the sun hot on your neck and no sound but the offended chattering of the local gopher, followed by the satisfying snap of the pod as you break it open and scoop out the little green pearls.

Fresh peas are the essence of summer. When steamed, with butter and a wisp of sugar, nothing is better.

There is also nothing better than picking and shelling your own. But when it isn't possible, some good brands of tiny frozen peas are on the market, and if you get there early, farmers markets will have fresh peas during the too-brief season.

IN THE MARKET: There are two kinds of peas available now. Shelling peas include those fat green pearls everybody grows, and *petit pois,* a variety of French peas that are tiny and sweet, with the most delicate flavor you can imagine.

Edible pod peas include the oriental snow peas (look for Snowflake and Norli) with delicately thin-walled pods and sugar snap peas (Sugar Mel and Sugar Ann) with thick, sweet, juicy pods.

Edible pods make excellent stir-fries, and for obvious reasons, are known in France as *mange toute.*

They're easy to grow and do well in cool weather. For the past several summers, I've grown mine along a wire fence, and the moment they reach the top, our resident squirrels begin to harvest them. It's a running battle – me against the wildlife.

▪ *Nutrition:* Good source of vitamins A and C; excellent fiber. About 95 calories per cup (250 mL) for fresh peas, 60 for edible pod peas.

Peas with Conchigliette and Cream

Spring Vegetable Potpie

Salad of Tiny Peas and Lettuce with Herbs and Bacon

■ ***Season:*** The best shelling peas are always the ones in your own garden, from late June to late August in most places. Edible pod varieties are available almost year-round.

■ ***Buy:*** One pound (500 g), unshelled, will give you about a cup (250 mL), shelled. Buy about 4 oz (115 g) of edible pod peas per person.

IN THE KITCHEN: Store peas in a plastic bag, refrigerated, for no more than 3 days.

Peas are one of those vegetables that are so delectable when steamed and served with no more than a good bash of butter and a speck of salt or a wisp of sugar, that it seems almost a sacrilege to do anything else.

If you feel compelled to tart them up with anything, a little freshly chopped mint or a few minced chives are acceptable, as is fresh dill and a discreet scoop of sour cream.

Or simply serve them with marble-sized new potatoes and baby carrots, all in the same dish and lavished with butter. Perfection!

Peas with Conchigliette and Cream

I could live on this fast, easy, comforting dish. Because of their shape, the conchigliette (little pasta shells) capture the sauce and peas, making a perfect conveyance from plate to mouth. The dish is best made with garden peas, but in winter when you can't get fresh peas, the tiny frozen ones are fine. Serve a salad on the side and a loaf of good bread.

Serves 4 as a main course

1 lb	conchigliette	500 g
3 cups	tiny shelled peas	750 mL
1 tbsp	butter	15 mL
6	thin slices prosciutto, finely diced	6
2 cups	half-and-half cream	500 mL
1 cup	freshly grated Asiago, Pedano, or Parmesan cheese	250 mL
	fresh pepper	
1/4 cup	fresh basil leaves, minced	50 mL

□ Bring a large pot of lightly salted water to a rolling boil. Cook pasta about 3 minutes, or until the shells have begun to soften. Add peas to the pot and after it returns to a boil, continue cooking 4 minutes for fresh peas, 2 minutes for frozen. Drain.

Melt butter in a large frying pan. Add the diced prosciutto and cook about 1 minute. Add the cream. As soon as it simmers, add the drained pasta and peas. Remove from heat, add the grated cheese, a good grinding of pepper, and the minced basil leaves. Toss quickly and serve in hot pasta bowls.

Spring Vegetable Potpie

This dish has other vegetables in it, but it's mostly about peas. A crisp, golden, double-puff pastry crust conceals a melange of spring vegetables bathed in parsley-scented cream. If you can't get fresh peas that have been picked that morning, use tiny frozen peas. The flavor of the edible pod peas will prop up the flavor.

Serves 4 to 6

1	14.5 oz (411 g) pkg puff pastry	1
12	tiny new potatoes	12
12	baby carrots	12
3 cups	shelled peas	750 mL
1 cup	snow peas, halved	250 mL
2 tbsp	butter	30 mL
2 tbsp	flour	30 mL
1 cup	half-and-half cream	250 mL
	reserved cooking liquid	
	salt and pepper	
1/4 cup	fresh parsley, minced	50 mL
1	egg	1
1 tbsp	water	15 mL

☐ Thaw pastry according to package directions. Cut in half. On a lightly floured board, roll each piece into a circle about 1 inch (2.5 cm) larger than the casserole. Reserve scraps to decorate crust. Cover and chill.

Wash potatoes and carrots well, but do not peel. Put potatoes and carrots in a large saucepan with about 1 inch

(2.5 cm) of water. Bring to a boil, cover, and cook about 5 minutes, or until vegetables are barely tender-crisp. Add peas and snow peas, and continue cooking about 3 minutes more. Drain, reserving cooking water.

Pour vegetables into a buttered 3 quart (3 L) casserole.

In the saucepan, melt butter over medium heat. Add flour and stir, cooking about 2 minutes. Add cream and stir briskly. Pour reserved vegetable juices into a measuring cup and add water to make 1 cup (250 mL). Add to sauce and continue stirring until smooth and slightly thickened. Season with salt and pepper. Stir in parsley. Pour over vegetables in casserole.

Make egg wash by beating egg with 1 tbsp (15 mL) cold water. Brush rim of casserole with egg wash and fit one circle of puff pastry over it. Brush crust lightly with egg wash and fit second crust over top. Crimp the overhanging edge, pulling it up to form an attractive rim. Decorate the crust with pastry leaves and petals cut from reserved pastry scraps. Brush crust with egg wash. Cut four small slits in the pastry for steam to escape.

(Continued on page 166)

Spring Vegetable Potpie

(Continued from page 165)

Bake casserole at 400 F (200 C) for 25 to 30 minutes, or until puffed and golden brown. Serve at once. This is delicious with salmon, chicken, or lamb chops and a salad of mixed greens in the simplest possible vinaigrette. Drink a cool, white wine and finish with strawberries dipped in yogurt and brown sugar.

Salad of Tiny Peas and Lettuce with Herbs and Bacon

If fresh peas are not available, use tiny frozen peas. The crisp texture of iceberg lettuce lightens the creamy dressing in this salad, which goes perfectly with an omelet, grilled fish, or chicken.

Serves 6

4 cups	tiny peas	1 L
2 cups	shredded iceberg lettuce	500 mL
6	red radishes, thinly sliced	6
3	slices bacon, cooked crisp	3
1/4 cup	chives, minced	50 mL
1/4 cup	dill, minced	50 mL
1/2 cup	light mayonnaise	125 mL
1/2 cup	skim milk yogurt	125 mL
	salt and pepper	

☐ Steam fresh peas in very little water for 5 minutes or less, just until they turn bright jade green. Run cold water through them to stop the cooking. Drain.

Put peas in a glass salad bowl. Top with iceberg lettuce, radishes, and bacon.

Stir together the chives, dill, mayonnaise, and yogurt. Season with salt and pepper. Pour over vegetables and toss lightly, until combined.

Chapter 27 ▪ Peppers

IN THE BIG CENTRAL FARMERS MARKET IN BUDAPEST THERE ARE MORE than a dozen kiosks devoted entirely to peppers.

For some reason, the pepper merchants are tucked away in a dim section of the sprawling market, but it doesn't matter because the red, orange, and yellow peppers glow in the permanent twilight as though they were electric. The pepper women know how wonderful their peppers look, and they festoon them across the booths like Christmas tree lights, dangle strings of them from the ceiling, drape them up and down and around, and pile them in every conceivable nook and cranny of the booth.

I think of them in autumn when peppers of every shape, size, and color come into the markets here at home.

IN THE MARKET: There are hundreds of different varieties of peppers grown around the world, ranging from sweet-as-apples to searing hot. And that's the simplest division – sweet and hot.

Sweet peppers, or at least mild peppers, tend to be larger than their hot cousins. Some are oblong or round, some are short and squat; others, like the thin-walled, Italian frying peppers and the meatier, waxy, Hungarian sweet yellows, are long and tapered.

A new one, which I've seen only once, is the amazing Chocolate Bell. Like most peppers, it starts out green but ripens to a lovely chocolate color with salmon-pink flesh and big yellow seeds.

Hot peppers are generally known simply as chilies, and they range from the long, tapering red or green Anaheim, the mildest of all, to the tiny, searing Scotch bonnets, which are hot enough to make your ears smoke.

Tapenade of Sweet Peppers and Sun-Dried Tomatoes

Embered Peppers, Sicilian Style

Twice-Grilled Annaheim Peppers with Cheese

Hot 'n Sweet Pepper Jam

Chilies require special handling because they contain capsaicin, a volatile phenolic compound that concentrates in the seeds and in the fibrous membranes that hold the seeds. The cook should take care to wear rubber gloves when handling chilies or at least to wash hands well in soapy water immediately after. Absolutely avoid touching the lips or eyes when working with these fiery little vegetables.

Meanwhile, the very stuff that can cause such painful burns can also heal, and medical research has found that it is useful as a blood thinner, to dissolve clots, and to reduce the level of harmful LDL cholesterol in some cases.

■ *Nutrition:* Peppers are one of the most nutrient-dense vegetables, high in amino acids, potassium, and a good source of other minerals. They're also higher in vitamin C than oranges, grapefruit, or tomatoes, with red ones having twice as much as green ones.

Although red peppers have a few more calories than green (50 in a large red bell as opposed to 35 in a large green bell), they also have a good supply of vitamin A.

■ *Season:* The big sweet bell peppers are at their peak throughout the summer months. Tiny imported chilies are available almost year-round but not always when you want them. Dried chilies make a good alternative.

■ *Buy:* For stuffing, allow one medium pepper per person.

IN THE KITCHEN: Unwashed peppers of any variety will keep in a perforated plastic bag, refrigerated, for 3 to 5 days. Once they've been cut, however, they deteriorate quickly. If you have leftover sliced peppers, plan to use them in a cooked dish as soon as possible.

Sweet peppers need to be washed and seeded, and they're ready to eat raw. Roasting them and then peeling the roasted skin off deepens and intensifies their flavor.

For how to roast hot peppers, see note immediately before the recipes.

Tapenade of Sweet Peppers and Sun-Dried Tomatoes

Another version of this nontraditional tapenade appeared in my second cookbook, the *Best of Seasons: Menu Cookbook.* I've increased the garlic and omitted the sugar in this one, which gives it a slightly louder flavor and makes full use of the sweetness in the tomatoes.

Tapenade is a delicious spread for toasted baguettes or as a pizza topping. If you want to buy roasted or grilled peppers packed in oil, both Primo and Unico pack a good version, and Italian delis sell them in bulk. Be sure they have been roasted rather than steamed (look for little telltale bits of charred skin).

Makes approximately 2 cups (500 mL)

1 cup	dry-pack sun-dried tomatoes	250 mL
3	red bell peppers, seeded, roasted, and skinned	3
1 tbsp	fruity olive oil	15 mL
1	medium onion, chopped	1
3 to 4	cloves garlic, pressed	3 to 4
2	ripe tomatoes, peeled and chopped	2
1 tbsp	balsamic vinegar	15 mL
1 tbsp	fresh oregano	15 mL
	or	
1 tsp	dried oregano	5 mL
1 cup	ripe olives, minced	250 mL
1/2 cup	fresh parsley, chopped	125 mL
	salt and coarse black pepper	

☐ Put sun-dried tomatoes in a small bowl and cover with hot water. Leave about 5 minutes, then drain. This will get rid of any excess salt on the tomatoes and start plumping them. Chop coarsely or snip with kitchen scissors.

Cut bell peppers into chunks.

In a large frying pan, heat oil. Add sun-dried tomatoes, peppers, onion, garlic, and ripe tomatoes. Cook about 2 minutes over medium heat.

Add vinegar and oregano. Turn heat to high and cook about 5 minutes more, until most of the liquid has evaporated.

Remove from heat and cool slightly. Spoon into a food processor and puree coarsely, using on-off bursts.

Stir in minced olives and parsley. Spoon into a glass jar . Store, covered and refrigerated, for no longer than two weeks. May be frozen.

Embered Peppers, Sicilian Style

I admit it. Most of the time, red, yellow, and orange bell peppers are a shocking price. You almost need to take out a loan to buy six of them, but they're rich in vitamins, and the red ones contain a whopping amount of vitamin C.

Although green bell peppers are fine in this dish when the budget can't accommodate the more expensive ones, this is most beautiful when made with red, yellow, and orange peppers. Like the oranges in Monet's painting or the peppers in the darker reaches of Budapest's central farmers market, they seem to glow with their own light.

Serve the peppers as part of an antipasto table or for a summer lunch with feta cheese and crusty bread.

Serves 6 to 8

3	red bell peppers	3
2	yellow bell peppers	2
1	orange bell pepper	1
3	cloves garlic, pressed	3
1 cup	olive oil	250 mL

☐ Cut peppers in half. Remove seeds and stem. Grill, skin side down over hot coals, until skins char. Remove with tongs and seal in a brown paper bag for 10 minutes, or until cool enough to handle. Rub off skin under cold running water. Pat dry. (If using a broiler in your kitchen, grill them skin side up.)

Slice pepper halves once again, lengthwise, so they're quartered. Lay in a platter with a lip. Stir the pressed garlic into the olive oil and pour it over the peppers, turning them so that every bit of surface is well-acquainted with the oil. Refrigerate for about three hours or as long as 1 week. Bring to room temperature before serving.

Embered peppers go well with crusty bread, as part of an antipasto table or a salad. Be sure to save the oil, which will have been infused with the pepper juices as well as the garlic. It's delicious as a salad oil or a brushing oil for bruschetta or croutons.

Grilled Cheese Variation: Slice a crusty baguette or Italian loaf lengthwise, cover with grated mozzarella cheese and slices of the peppers. Sprinkle lightly with freshly grated Parmesan. Bake at 450 F (230 C) until cheese bubbles nicely. Cut in generous chunks.

Twice-Grilled Annaheim Peppers with Cheese

Sweet but pungent Annaheims are first grilled to enhance their own flavor, then stuffed with a generous chunk of cheese and grilled again until the cheese becomes meltingly soft. Sweet Hungarian yellow peppers can also be used.

Serves 4

8	large Annaheim chilies	8
8	chunks mozzarella cheese, to fit peppers	8
	olive oil	

☐ Grill or broil peppers, turning once, until skins are charred. Remove with tongs and seal in a paper bag for about 10 minutes. Rub skins off under cold running water, taking care not to tear the flesh. Pat dry. Snip out the stem end and as much membrane and seeds as possible, taking care not to split the flesh. At this point they can be covered and refrigerated until just before serving.

Meanwhile, cut the cheese so it's about 1/2 inch (1.25 cm) thick and as long and wide as will fit comfortably inside the peppers.

To finish cooking, stuff each pepper with cheese, being careful not to tear the flesh. Brush peppers with olive oil and return to the hot grill. Cook on both sides, turning once, just until cheese has melted. Serve warm with good bread, as an appetizer or a light lunch.

Hot 'n Sweet Pepper Jam

Herb grower, restaurant critic, and author Noel Richardson lives on Vancouver Island. Her kitchen overflows with cookbooks, herbs from her prolific gardens, cookbooks, dogs, cats, and a steady stream of wonderful food.

The inspiration for this jam came from her pepper jam. I've taken liberties by adding yellow peppers and zapping in a few jalapenos. It's delicious with tiny hot biscuits slathered with whipped cream cheese.

This is an expensive jam to make due to the price of red peppers, so I pack it in small jars and make a big deal of serving it to only those deserving friends who need special pampering.

Makes 2 cups (500 mL)

4	red bell peppers	4
4	yellow bell peppers	4
5	red or partly green jalapenos	5
1 1/2 tbsp	salt	22.5 mL
1 cup	red wine vinegar	250 mL
2 cups	sugar	500 mL
6	thin slices fresh ginger, minced	6

☐ Slice, seed, and coarsely grind peppers, including the jalapenos. This can be done in an old-fashioned meat grinder or by using on-off bursts in a processor, but take care not to overprocess.

Put ground peppers in a glass bowl, sprinkle with salt, and let it sit overnight in the refrigerator.

In the morning, drain the liquid, reserving half and returning it to the peppers.

Transfer peppers to an enamel or pyrex saucepan. Add vinegar, sugar, and ginger. Bring to a boil, then immediately reduce to simmer.

Simmer for one hour, stirring frequently, until mixture is thick and glossy. Pour into small, sterilized jars and seal with paraffin.

This jelly will keep, refrigerated, for up to 3 months, says Noel.

(Not mine. It's all down the hatch long before that.)

Chapter 28 ▪ Potatoes

I COULD WRITE A BOOK ABOUT POTATOES. IN FACT, A POEM. AN ENTIRE sonnet, maybe.

The thing is, I love them. *Adore* them. For some people, chocolate is the great comforter. For me, you can lose the chocolate and give me a baked potato, one with well-scrubbed skin so I can eat that, too. A blob of butter, a speck of salt and pepper, and I'm in heaven.

Or in those rare moments when I'm feeling thin enough to indulge, I want nothing more than a big scoop of oily French fries, sprinkled with salt and doused with vinegar, served in a cut-off brown paper bag so they steam a little and get positively juicy.

Then there are those marble-sized babies with the crisp red skin, which snaps when you sink your teeth into it, and the pots of whipped russets, and the leftovers, fried with onions. And so forth.

IN THE MARKET: Some potatoes have delicate skin, so thin and tender when they're young that the gentlest rub takes it off. Their flesh is waxy and they're at their best boiled, steamed, or just butter-smothered until they're barely tender, which takes all of 10 minutes to do.

Others, the russet or baking type, have thicker skins and a dryer texture known as mealy.

But that's only scratching the surface. There are hundreds of varieties of this useful tuber. Very few make it to the commercial market, but many small growers are so enchanted with the colors, sizes, shapes, and textures yielded by their trial plots that they bring a few into their early morning market stalls for the pleasure of discerning customers. At your farmers market, look for Russian or Belgian Banana potatoes, small, fingerling-sized spuds with sweet,

New Potatoes with Dill Butter Sauce

Lillianna's Oven-Roasted Potatoes

Red Potato Puree

Potato Cakes with Wild Rice

Whipped Potatoes with Spinach

Grilled Sweet Potatoes

ivory-colored flesh and delicate skin, or the similarly shaped Yellow Finn or Ruby Crescent, a stubby, rosy-skinned potato. Then there's Yukon gold, a potato with pale, yellow flesh and a delicately buttery flavor.

Although the flavors of various novelty potatoes vary from earthy to sweet to faintly mineral, the flavor differences aren't a patch on the color variations. Novelty potatoes come in a rainbow of colors, all the way from the buttery yellow flesh of the Yellow Finn to the pink-fleshed Levitt's Pink, the red-fleshed All Red, and the nearly indigo All Blue. Most of the new varieties hold their color well after cooking and can turn a prosaic potato salad into a rainbow.

■ *Note:* Avoid potatoes that are green. Due to careless storage, potatoes are sometimes exposed to too much light, which produces the toxic substance known as *solanine*. If you discover it after you get them home, cut into one to see how far the green extends. If it's only a thin layer, it can be pared off. Otherwise, take them back.

■ *Nutrition:* High in vitamin C and potassium, low in fat and sodium. Good source of easily used iron and complex carbohydrates. One large potato with skin has about 170 calories (without the toppings).

■ *Season:* Haunt the markets or befriend a grower so you can enjoy the marble-sized baby spuds that appear in late June through July and early August. Thin-skinned potatoes are available until frost in northern regions and from southern markets year-round. Russets are harvested in September and keep well until spring.

■ *Buy:* One large baking potato, 3 banana potatoes or fingerlings, or 4 to 5 baby potatoes per person.

IN THE KITCHEN: It's important to keep potatoes cool but not cold. Store them in a dark, ventilated place. Never store potatoes in tight plastic bags or you'll end up with rotten spuds.

New Potatoes with Dill Butter Sauce

Cooking doesn't get any simpler than this, and eating doesn't get any better.

These delicious potatoes are only possible during the few weeks of spring when gardeners are willing to steal them from the side of the hills before they have a chance to mature.

I use the round red skinned potatoes for this dish, but red or yellow fingerlings such as Yellow Finn or Ruby Crescent are wonderful. Fresh dill is essential.

Serves 6

2 lbs	baby potatoes	1 kg
1/2 cup	water	125 mL
1/2 cup	butter	125 mL
1/4 cup	fresh dillweed	50 mL
	salt and pepper	

☐ Scrub potatoes just until clean, leaving as much of the skin as possible.

Put potatoes in a medium pot with water and butter. Bring to a boil and cook, covered, until just tender, about 10 minutes. Drain. Add dillweed to the pot and shake back and forth several times. Season lightly with salt and pepper. Serve immediately.

Sour Cream Variation: For a special celebration, serve these potatoes with a bowl of sour cream, freshly chopped chives, and a little pot of the best caviar you can afford, if you love caviar (many people don't). Or forget the caviar and just go with the sour cream and chives. Yum.

Embered Baby Spuds Variation: Omit the butter. Steam potatoes only 5 minutes, then thread onto skewers. Brush with olive oil and grill over hot coals until just tender, turning several times. Serve sour cream (and caviar, if that's the league you're in) on the side.

Lillianna's Oven-Roasted Potatoes

One summer Ed and I stayed for a while in an old house south of Florence, in the Chianti Classico region of Italy. The property came with mice, olive trees, a vineyard, Sergio (keeper of olives, maker of wine), a flock of chickens, a little black rooster, and one mean-tempered goose. Lillianna, a cook who spoke no English but communicated through her excellent cooking, was part of the deal.

These potatoes, oven-roasted with peppers and onions in a fruity olive oil, were one of her specialties. They grow crusty on the outside, like you always hope French fries will be. Lillianna served them with roast chicken, but they go well with any grilled meat.

Serves 4

4	large russet-type potatoes, scrubbed	4
1	large onion, peeled	1
1	large green bell pepper, sliced	1
1/2 cup	extra-virgin olive oil	125 mL
	salt	

☐ Slice potatoes lengthwise into six or eight sections. Slice onion and pepper lengthwise into sixths. Coat a medium-sized roaster with olive oil. Put vegetables in the roaster and drizzle with oil. Add salt and toss to distribute the oil so it touches all surfaces. Cover and bake at 350 F (180 C) for about 25 minutes. Remove cover, stir vegetables, and continue roasting until brown and crisp.

Onion Soup Variation: Potatoes with onion soup is an old trick but a tasty one. Omit the salt in the above combination and sprinkle with an envelope of dehydrated onion soup. Roast, uncovered, at 425 F (220 C) for about 45 minutes, stirring now and then so nothing burns and all the flavors get acquainted.

Red Potato Puree

My grandmother taught me that the only potato to mash was a russet type.

For once, Grandma was wrong. The small, round, red potatoes of early summer, boiled with their skins on and mashed with a sinful amount of butter and cream, are one of the most delicious things in the western world, bar none. The bits of new potato skin add marvelous texture and flavor, and then there's the butter and cream. Yum. All they need is a speck of salt and a grinding of fresh pepper, and heaven is at hand. Serve with a roast of veal au jus and creamed baby spinach. Drink a young, fruity Beaujolais. Perfection.

Serves 6 to 8

2 lbs	red potatoes, scrubbed	1 kg
1/2 cup	butter	125 mL
1/2 cup	whipping cream	125 mL
	salt and pepper	

☐ Boil potatoes in their skins until tender. Drain all but 1/2 cup (125 mL) of the cooking water. Mash potatoes into the cooking water in the pot, and then beat with an electric mixer turned on low, gradually adding butter and cream until the potatoes are fluffy. Season to taste.

Carrot Variation: Add 6 small, young carrots, scrubbed but not peeled, to the potato pot and cook together. Drain, reserving cooking liquid. Return liquid to the pot and continue boiling until reduced to about 1/2 cup (125 mL). Proceed as above.

Cream Cheese and Chive Variation: To the cooked, drained potatoes, add 8 oz (250 g) light cream cheese, cubed, 1 clove garlic, pressed, and 1/2 cup (125 mL) freshly chopped chives. Whip as above, omitting the butter and cream.

Potato Cakes with Wild Rice

Use either leftover or freshly prepared potatoes and cooked wild rice for this dish. It is superb with any salmon dish, fresh peas, and a salad of mixed leaf lettuces. Both the potatoes and the wild rice can be cooked well ahead of time, and the cakes formed, covered, and refrigerated until you're ready to cook them.

Makes 8 cakes

3 cups	Red Potato Puree (see recipe above)	750 mL
1	green onion, finely minced	1
1 cup	cooked wild rice	250 mL
1	egg, beaten	1
	salt and pepper	
1 tbsp	vegetable oil	15 mL
1/4 cup	butter	50 mL

☐ In a medium bowl, mix together potato puree, onion, rice, egg, salt, and pepper.

Rub your hands with a bit of oil and form 1/2 cup (125 mL) portions into small, flat patties.

In a large frying pan, heat oil and butter together over medium heat until the butter foams. Add the flattened potato cakes and cook until golden brown. With a spatula, turn the cakes and brown on the other side. Keep hot until the salmon is ready.

Whipped Potatoes with Spinach

While the potatoes are thoroughly cooked and whipped to a creamy softness, the fresh, raw spinach beaten into the hot puree retains its brilliant color and adds an earthy flavor to this simple dish.

Serves 6 to 8

6	large russet type potatoes, peeled	6
1 cup	milk, heated	250 mL
1/4 cup	butter	50 mL
	salt and white pepper	
1 cup	spinach leaves, torn	250 mL
	additional butter, as needed	
	nutmeg *(optional)*	

☐ Boil potatoes until tender. Drain, reserving about 1/2 cup (125 mL) of the cooking water. With the potatoes in the reserved water, mash with a potato masher. Add milk, butter, salt, and pepper, and beat until fluffy.

Add torn spinach leaves into the pot with the potatoes and stir vigorously. The heat will turn the leaves a brilliant jade and release a wonderful earthy flavor.

Serve immediately with additional butter. A wisp of nutmeg may be added to these potatoes along with the spinach.

Broccoli Bacon Variation: Omit spinach. Instead, add 2 slices crisp-fried bacon, crumbled, and 1 cup (250 mL) cooked broccoli, finely chopped, to the drained potatoes. Beat with a spoon until fluffy. Turn into a buttered casserole, sprinkle with grated Parmesan cheese, and bake in a 400 F (200 C) oven about 10 minutes, or until just golden brown.

Grilled Sweet Potatoes

The ongoing discussion over yam versus sweet potato is of little consequence when yams are so seldom in the markets. For this dish, use large sweet potatoes. They'll glaze to a rich mahogany color with a crusty exterior and meltingly soft flesh.

Serves 8

4	large sweet potatoes	4
1/2 cup	soy sauce	125 mL
1/4 cup	molasses	50 mL
1 tbsp	vinegar	15 mL
2 tbsp	canola oil	30 mL
	salt and pepper	

☐ In a large pot, cover unpeeled potatoes with salted water and bring to a boil. Cook about 30 minutes, or until barely tender. Drain. When cool enough to handle, slice lengthwise. Cut a thin slice off the bottom side of each half, just so it will sit on a grill.

Combine remaining ingredients in a jar and shake vigorously. Brush cut surfaces of potatoes generously with sauce. Let potatoes rest about 10 minutes, then brush again.

Place on an oiled grill over a hot fire. Cook for about 3 minutes on cut side. Brush once again with marinade and turn, grilling the bottom side about 5 minutes. Serve hot.

Chapter 29
Pumpkin and Winter Squash

THE SQUASH FAMILY IS A LARGE AND FUNNY-LOOKING BROOD, RANGING from long, lean, and green to short, fat, and golden. You've got your hard-shell or winter and your soft-shell or summer.

Winter squash is meaty, but the flavor is so delicate that it almost isn't there at all so a little help is in order. If you want to buy by the chunk, look for the slightly sweet Banana squash or the even sweeter Hubbard, a warty-looking giant ranging from grey-green to orange to dark green. A large Japanese variety, the grey-green Hokkaido, has a drier texture and a buttery flavor. Then there's the yellow-skinned, pear-shaped Butternut, the ever-popular Acorn squash, or the sweet little Dumpling. A smallish winter squash with lovely dark stripes on a yellow background is the Delicata; the flesh is sweet and tender, and it's perfect for stuffing. Look for Sugarloaf Delicata, an even smaller one.

Beyond these are so many more: the Ebony acorn, which is nearly black, the Kabocha, the Buttercup. Stuff them, stew them, turn them into pies. Winter squash makes a most obliging companion for spices and herbs, onions and tomatoes, bacon, ham, and almost any meat you wish to use as a stuffing.

Pumpkin is the noblest, nicest squash of all. It has inspired an organization known as the World Pumpkin Confederation, headquartered in New York and dedicated to the "hobby sport" of giant pumpkin production. With branches in 30 countries, the great pumpkins are a hot topic every October.

In a village near my home, the Smoky Lake Pumpkin Growers hold their annual giant pumpkin competition. For weeks before the weigh-off, the population of Smoky Lake watches and waits. One grower builds giant smudges to ward off frost, hauling poplar logs into his garden and laying a

Pumpkin Soup

Pumpkin Stew with Jamaican Meatballs

Acorn Squash with Cheddar and Peppers

Butternut Squash with Sweet Tomato Chutney

blanket of smoke over the entire town. Another grower, fearing for the welfare of his best plant, builds a permanent greenhouse right over top of the vine. And so it goes.

On the day of the big weigh-off, fans come from miles around and pack the local arena an hour before the show starts. Tension mounts as the giant squash are lugged from the back of pickups and vans onto the stage, jostled into position on the scale, and weighed.

At first the crowd continues to chatter. Two farmers behind me discuss the harvest (bad), the economy (sad), and the present government (useless). But as the weights are toted up, all eyes are on the stage where the huge competitors are vying for the prize. When the winner is announced at a bouncing 369 lb (167 kg), a cheer goes up.

"Damn!" cries the astonished farmer behind me. "That squash is bigger 'n a hog!"

Meanwhile, a special phone line links Smoky Lake to the World Pumpkin Weigh-off Headquarters in New York where the championship will be decided. It's not unusual to have pumpkins weighing 500 lbs grown from the seed called Atlantic Giant.

And giants they are, oddballs in the vegetable world, more yellow than orange, with pale, fibrous flesh and many seeds, which will be carefully saved. They aren't always the classic pumpkin shape, and they don't even make great pies. But it doesn't matter. In the hobby sport of giant pumpkins, the weight's the thing.

IN THE MARKET: Winter squash: Markets in France and Italy sell pumpkins by the wedge, but it's a different sort of pumpkin than our jack-o'-lantern type. Flattish and deeply ridged, with thick skin ranging from brown to deep orange, the flesh is such an intense color that it almost glows. If you're buying by the wedge, look for Rouge d'Etampe among the elite of the pumpkin crowd. It's a grand soup pumpkin, and it bakes beautifully.

The other approach for the cook is to go the whole pumpkin route, in which case you need a large, symmetrical pumpkin, one of the Cinderella's coach models that have been bred for their gorgeous round shape, brilliant orange color, and thick, sweet flesh. They have enchanting names: Spooky, Autumn Gold, Ghost Rider.

For the smaller appetite and those who want a pumpkin for every guest at your table, there are miniatures like Baby Bear, Thumbelina, and Jack Be Little. They can be steamed whole, hollowed slightly, and piled with a savory stuffing of rice or meat.

■ *Nutrition:* Winter squash is an excellent source of vitamin A, low in sodium, ranges from about 90 to 130 calories per cup (250 mL), cooked.

from The Garden

- **Season:** Although most winter squash peaks from September through late winter, many hard-shell squash such as Acorn, Spaghetti squash, Hubbard, and Banana are available year-round.

- **Buy:** 6 oz (170 g) of cut squash per person, half an Acorn or Dumpling, or a whole mini-pumpkin.

IN THE KITCHEN: The joy of winter squash is that they're great keepers, and they make such handsome ornaments during the keeping.

I'm especially crazy about the multicolored Turbans, which can be bright orange on the bottom, green-and-white striped on the top, and look more like the headgear of an ancient wealthy Turk than a vegetable.

Pumpkins by the back door, a giant Hubbard squash on the landing, and a few Dumplings or Acorns in a wooden bowl make their own beautiful still life. When you're ready to eat them, an hour in the oven will, as one of my favorite garden writers says, "melt the hard flesh, releasing the stored, sun-ripened sweetness."

Pumpkin Soup

Pumpkin soup belongs to Thanksgiving, Halloween, and those other autumn and winter occasions when you want to honor tradition while feasting. This one is based on the classic French *potage au potiron,* but I've taken several liberties, and this simplified soup, which gets a flavor jolt from the addition of medium or hot salsa, would have the old French cooks spinning in their graves.

Salsa? Zut, alors! C'est impossible! C'est criminale!

Too bad they'll never know what they missed.

We serve this soup in a large, hollowed-out pumpkin for Thanksgiving, especially if children are at the table, as they find the glorious color and lovely shape enchanting. So do I.

Although canned pumpkin may certainly be used here, it's fun to do it from scratch, starting the day before, baking the diced pumpkin meat in the oven until it's soft and tender, before mashing it, and building up to the grand finale the next day.

(Continued on page 186)

Pumpkin Tureen

For a smashing presentation, cut a lid out of the top of a handsome, tureen-sized pumpkin (about 12 lbs / 6 kg). Clean out the seeds and stringy bits. Place pumpkin shell in a cake pan and put it on the bottom rack of a 325 F (160 C) oven. Fill the pumpkin with boiling water. Replace lid and bake about 1 hour, or until the inner flesh is barely tender.

Ladle as much water as possible out of the pumpkin. Using oven mitts, turn the shell over and drain it well. Wipe the shell with cooking oil, just to give it a lovely glow.

Place it on a suitable platter or tray, and surround it with green leaves and bunches of red berries. Wisps of cedar and bunches of mountain ash or bittersweet look wonderful.

Carefully pour the soup into the tureen and serve it forth. Scoop a little pumpkin meat out with each ladle of soup, being careful not to scoop too deep – your tureen might spring a leak.

Cheese pastry straws or thin, crisp, herbed breadsticks are good with this as are thin slices of French bread brushed with olive oil, rubbed with garlic, and baked in a slow oven until crisp.

Pumpkin Soup

(Continued from page 186)

Serves 8 to 10

2 tbsp	butter	30 mL
1	small onion, diced	1
1 tbsp	flour	15 mL
4 cups	chicken broth	1 L
3 cups	cooked, mashed pumpkin	750 mL
1 tbsp	brown sugar	15 mL
1 tsp	cinnamon	5 mL
1/2 tsp	cumin	2 mL
1/2 cup	medium or hot salsa	125 mL
1 1/2 tsp	salt	7 mL
1 cup	half-and-half cream, scalded	250 mL
1 to 2 tbsp	cilantro, minced	15 to 30 mL
	cilantro leaves for garnish	

☐ In a Dutch oven over medium heat, melt butter and sauté onion until transparent. Sprinkle with flour and cook until bubbly.

Reduce to simmer and add chicken stock gradually, stirring with a wire whisk.

Add pumpkin, sugar, cinnamon, cumin, salsa, and salt, whisking to blend.

While mixture is still simmering, whisk in the scalded half-and-half.

Taste the soup and correct the seasoning. Stir in minced cilantro. Serve with a cilantro leaf floating in each bowl.

Pumpkin Stew with Jamaican Meatballs

The original version of this stew was a prize winner in a contest I ran in the Edmonton Journal one Halloween. It's been adapted with a mixture of beef and pork and a good smash of Jamaican jerk seasoning in the meatballs.

Pumpkin stew is a good dish for the day after Halloween when you have fresh pumpkin meat hanging around with nowhere important to go. Like the pumpkin soup, this stew can also be served in a pumpkin shell for a party.

Serves 6

1 lb	lean ground beef	500 g
1/2 lb	lean ground pork	250 g
1 tbsp	Jamaican jerk seasoning	15 mL
1	clove garlic, pressed	1
1	small onion, minced	1
1 cup	soft bread crumbs	250 mL
1	egg	1
2 lb	pumpkin meat	1 kg
1	medium onion, diced	1
1	stalk celery, diced	1
	salt and pepper	
1 1/2 cups	Cheddar cheese, grated	375 mL
1	19 oz (540 mL) can tomatoes	1
	sour cream, diced green onion for garnish	

☐ Mix together meats, seasonings, garlic, minced onion, bread crumbs, and egg. Form into meatballs the size of walnuts. Roll in a little flour and place on a non-stick cookie sheet. Bake at 400 F (200 C) for about 15 minutes, or until well browned.

Reduce oven to 350 F (180 C). Coat a 12 cup (3 L) casserole with non-stick spray. Peel and dice the pumpkin into 1/2 inch (1.25 cm) cubes. (The amount is not critical.) Place pumpkin in casserole along with diced onion and celery. Season with salt and pepper. Sprinkle with half the cheese. Top with baked meatballs.

Break up the tomatoes and pour them, with their juice, over the meatballs. Cover and bake 1 hour. Stir, add remaining cheese, and bake uncovered for 20 minutes more, or until pumpkin is tender.

This is delicious served over steamed rice, and garnished with sour cream and diced green onion.

Acorn Squash with Cheddar and Peppers

Stuffed squash halves are a lovely vegetable for Thanksgiving or any fall meal. Green or golden Acorn squash, the small sweet Dumpling, the Delicata, or the miniature pumpkins marketed as Munchkin or Jack Be Little, all work well for stuffing. Virtually any squash can be adapted to this recipe.

Serves 8

4	acorn squash, halved and steamed	4
1/2 cup	Cheddar cheese, grated	125 mL
1/2 cup	whipped salad dressing	125 mL
1	green onion, minced	1
3/4 cup	green bell pepper, minced	175 mL
	salt and pepper	

☐ Halve the squash, scoop out the seeds, then either bake, microwave, or steam in a little water until the flesh is very tender. Once cooked, let the squash cool until it can be handled. Scoop flesh out of the halves into a large bowl, reserving shells.

Combine squash with cheese, whipped salad dressing, green onion, green pepper, salt, and pepper. Beat with an electric mixer until fluffy. Scoop into squash shells, mounding slightly. This may be done ahead of time and refrigerated.

Thirty minutes before serving, put shells upright in an oven-proof dish. Add a little boiling water to the bottom of the dish and bake at 350 F (180 C) for about 30 minutes. Serve hot.

Jalapeno Cilantro Variation: Omit the green bell pepper. Fold in 1/2 cup ((125 mL) or more to taste, canned jalapeno peppers, minced, and 2 tbsp (30 mL) cilantro, minced. Garnish with cilantro sprigs.

Butternut Squash with Sweet Tomato Chutney

Although this recipe is wonderful with Butternut, it works equally well with traditional green or orange Hubbard, the striped Delicata, creamy Banana, Chestnut, or most of the Chinese or Japanese squash such as Green Hokkaido. Some of these squash are so big their size intimidates the cook, but most markets sell them in pieces, so buy only as much as you need.

Serves 6

2 lbs	butternut or other squash	1 kg
2 tbsp	soft butter	30 mL
	salt, pepper, freshly grated nutmeg	
1 cup	Sweet Tomato Chutney or chili sauce (see section on Tomatoes for recipe)	250 mL
1/2 cup	light sour cream	125 mL

☐ Pare and dice squash, and cook in boiling salted water until tender. Drain and mash with butter. Season with salt, pepper, and freshly grated nutmeg. Spread in a 8 cup (2 L) casserole.

Stir chutney and sour cream together and pour over squash. Run under broiler until bubbly, about 3 minutes.

Chapter 30 ■ Radish

WHEN I WAS A CHILD, MY MOTHER GREW WHITE ICICLE RADISHES. THEY were Burpees, and they came directly after the tiny red spring radishes, her French Breakfasts. She ate the icicles whole, dipped in a little mound of salt before each bite and accompanied by well-buttered bread. They were so crisp and juicy that eating them was a noisy business, and their flavor was at once peppery and mustardy.

It was her private snack, available only in spring before summer's heat made her beloved icicles strong and woody.

I doubt that she knew about the French fetish with *primeurs,* marble-sized red radishes, eaten on fresh, crusty bread that is first lavished with cold butter. She didn't have to know, good food was instinctive with her.

Radish history goes back further than the French, all the way to the ancient Chinese dynasties where both black and white winter radishes, earlier versions of those we know as daikon radishes, were cherished.

IN THE MARKET: Because there are two kinds of radish – the huge winter or oriental and the dainty, marble-shaped French that's at its best in spring – we enjoy them year-round.

I buy imported radishes in January for the same reason I buy tulips, to fend off the mid-winter blues. Sitting in my favorite chair with the dogs, eating radishes and my own homemade bread, and watching the blizzard howl is a special January pleasure for me. These imported radishes are red, sweet, and crisp with lots of juice, and they take well to grating.

But in the spring and summer markets, I look for smaller radishes in greater variety: tiny Cherry Belles, the lovely, multicolored Easter Eggs, the reliable, longish French Breakfast, and always some good old White Icicles.

Also available from radish fanciers are the new Purple Plum, big, purple-skinned globes with crisp, white flesh, and the late-summer Munchener Bier radish. Local growers of oriental vegetables will supply you with long, crisp daikon that look more like a white carrot and are apt to be sweeter, juicier and have better texture than imported daikon.

■ *Nutrition:* Very low in fat and calories; good source of vitamin C.

■ *Season:* Early spring into summer for French varieties; autumn and winter for German and oriental varieties. Imported radishes are available year-round.

■ *Buy:* Count on three or four small radishes per person. One medium daikon will serve 6 to 8.

IN THE KITCHEN: Unless you're using the tops to enhance presentation, as in salad baskets, cut the tops off to keep them from sapping the juices in the radish. Refrigerate summer varieties in plastic containers for about a week, oriental varieties for two weeks.

 _from The Garden_

Daikon on Rye

This is much like the traditional Octoberfest snack served in Munich's beer halls, but it's made with daikon, which is easier to find than beer radishes. It may seem too simple for words, or recipes, but don't underestimate the power of this little snack.

Serves 4

1	daikon radish	1
1/2 cup	cream cheese, softened	125 mL
1/2 cup	butter	125 mL
8	slices black or heavy rye bread	8
	salt	

☐ Peel and thinly slice the daikon radish. Whip together the cream cheese and butter. Spread on thinly sliced bread and cut in triangles. Cover each slice with overlapping slices of daikon. Salt lightly. Serve with mugs of beer.

Radish and Romaine Salad

In the late fall and winter, I often find large, imported red radishes, almost golf-ball size, that are not at all woody. They're perfect for grating coarsely and combining with a chiffonade of romaine and firm button mushrooms.

Serves 8

2 cups	red radishes, sliced	500 mL
2 cups	white button mushrooms, sliced	500 mL
8 to 10	large romaine leaves	8 to 10
4	green onions	4
	toasted sesame seeds	

Marinade

3 tbsp	rice vinegar	45 mL
1 tbsp	distilled vinegar	15 mL
1 tsp	brown sugar	5 mL
1 tsp	sesame oil	5 mL
2 tbsp	canola oil	30 mL
2 tbsp	soy sauce	30 mL
1 tsp	freshly grated ginger	5 mL
1	large clove garlic, pressed	1

☐ Using the coarse blade of a hand grater or with a food processor blade, grate the radishes as coarsely as possible. Slice the mushrooms.

Transfer grated radish and mushroom slices to 2 small bowls.

Put all ingredients for marinade in a small bowl and whisk together.

Divide marinade between radish and mushroom slices. Marinate for about 30 minutes.

Stack the romaine leaves, roll them into a long bundle, and cut across the bundle making thin spaghetti-like strips of romaine. (This is the chiffonade.) Lay romaine on a platter.

Slice green onions and sprinkle over romaine.

Drain mushrooms and radishes, reserving marinade.

Distribute mushrooms toward the center of the romaine, making a circle. Spoon radishes into the middle. Drizzle the romaine with some of the marinade. Sprinkle salad with toasted sesame seeds. Serve with salad tongs, and guests can mix the salad themselves.

Couscous Salad with Radishes and Peas

Instant couscous has its place and this is one of them. The
salad keeps well in the refrigerator for a couple of days,
improving in flavor on the second day as the herbs and
vinegar begin to perfume the grains of couscous.

Serves 8 to 10

1 1/2	cups chicken stock	375 mL
1 tbsp	olive oil	15 mL
1 cup	instant couscous	250 mL
12	red radishes, minced	12
2	green onions, minced	2
1 cup	tiny peas, fresh or frozen	250 mL
1/2 cup	fresh parsley, minced	125 mL
1/2 cup	cilantro, minced	125 mL
	cilantro leaves and whole red radishes for garnish	

Dressing

1/4 cup	white rice vinegar	50 mL
1/2 cup	olive oil	125 mL
1/2 tsp	ground ginger	2 mL
1/2 tsp	cumin	2 mL
	salt and pepper to taste	

□ In a medium pot, bring chicken stock and olive oil to a boil. Add couscous, stirring to prevent lumps. Immediately remove from heat. Cover and let rest 5 minutes. Fluff with a fork.

Add the vegetables and herbs. Combine dressing ingredients and pour over mixture. Toss lightly. Refrigerate 2 hours or up to 8 hours. Serve on a platter, garnished with cilantro leaves and small, whole red radishes with a few top leaves.

Chapter 31 ■ Spinach

IN THE MARKET: Spinach: During the winter months we see something called ice plant instead of summer spinach. It's a New Zealand version of the same plant, and although its leaves are coarser and the flavor less delicate, it's otherwise virtually identical.

■ *Nutrition:* Cooked spinach is high in iron. Raw or cooked, it's rich in vitamin A and potassium, and provides a good amount of vitamin C and riboflavin.

■ *Season:* Year-round in the markets. The quality has improved with the introduction of hydroponic growing, which produces a sweet tender leaf minus the grit. In May and June when the new crop of baby spinach comes into the local farmers market, I'm first in line.

■ *Buy:* 4 oz (115 g) per person, raw, 8 oz (250 g) per person if cooking the spinach.

IN THE KITCHEN: Discard any damaged or yellowed leaves. Tail the spinach by bending the stem backward across your index finger and drawing the stem along the leaf. This removes the strings at the same time. Wash and rinse, and rinse again. Wrap in paper towels, then in plastic. Refrigerate 2 to 3 days, but no longer.

Spinach Salad with Warm Croutons and Asiago Cheese

Spinach Ricotta Pies in Potato Bacon Crust

Spinach-Wrapped Cheese Grill

Spinach Salad with Warm Croutons and Asiago Cheese

There's quite a lot of bread in this very satisfying version of a traditional spinach salad. The big, warm garlic croutons and chunks of bacon grab onto the granular texture of the Asiago. They make a wonderful counterpoint to the fresh, mineral taste of spinach. It belongs to one of those growly spring evenings before Easter when the air still smells of winter.

Serves 6

6 cups	young spinach leaves	1.5 L
6	thick-cut slices bacon, coarsely diced	6
2	cloves garlic, pressed	2
12	thin baguette slices, halved	12
1/4 cup	balsamic vinegar	50 mL
1/2 cup	light olive oil	125 mL
1 tsp	dry mustard	5 mL
1/2 cup	Asiago cheese, grated	125 mL
	coarsely grated pepper	

☐ Wash spinach leaves thoroughly until no trace of grit remains. Tear coarsely into a large salad bowl.

Coat a cookie sheet with olive oil. Lay bacon on it. Scatter the garlic over it and muddle around with a wooden spoon until evenly distributed.

Place in a 400 F (200 C) oven and bake until bacon sizzles. Reduce heat to 350 F (180 C), lay baguette slices on top, and continue baking about 10 minutes, lifting and stirring the bread and bacon occasionally, turning it so all the surfaces are exposed to all the flavors.

When bread is toasted and bacon cooked, scoop into a heated bowl. Scrape bacon drippings into a small jar with balsamic vinegar, oil, and dry mustard. Shake vigorously.

Sprinkle warm croutons and bacon with grated Asiago. Toss.

Scoop bacon and croutons over spinach. Drizzle with balsamic mixture. Grate pepper over salad and toss. Serve immediately.

Spinach Ricotta Pies in Potato Bacon Crust

Spinach and ricotta cheese are a natural marriage, and the potato bacon crust is one of those delicious, finger-lickin' events that haunts the dreams of hungry dieters. The flavors of smoke and cheese belong more to winter than to any other season, but this also makes a splendid picnic dish to eat cold in the middle of July.

For convenience, I've used frozen spinach. Using a food processor to grate the potatoes speeds an otherwise tedious process.

Serves 6

Crust

3 cups	raw potato, grated	750 mL
1	small onion, grated	1
3	slices bacon, finely minced	3
1	egg, beaten	1
	salt and pepper	

☐ Generously butter 6 individual meat pie tins or oversized muffin tins, then coat with non-stick spray.

Spoon the grated potato onto a clean dish towel and wring it as hard as possible to remove excess liquid. Put potato in a medium bowl with onion, bacon, egg, and seasoning. Combine well.

Divide evenly into the pie tins, pressing the filling into the bottom and up the sides. Bake at 400 F (200 C) 25 minutes.

(Continued on page 198)

Spinach Ricotta Pies in Potato Bacon Crust

(Continued from page 197)

Filling

2 tbsp	butter	30 mL
2	12 oz (375 g) packages frozen spinach, chopped	2
2	cloves garlic, pressed	2
1 lb	ricotta cheese, drained	500 g
3	eggs, beaten	3
3 or 4 drops	hot pepper sauce	3 or 4 drops
2 tbsp	cornstarch	30 mL
1 tsp	salt	5 mL
	Parmesan cheese	

☐ In a large frying pan, melt butter. Add chopped spinach and garlic, and cook, stirring, until liquid evaporates.

In a medium bowl, mix cooked spinach, ricotta, eggs, pepper sauce, cornstarch, and salt, beating lightly with a wooden spoon, ensuring cheese is well combined.

Pour into potato crusts, dividing evenly and filling to the top. Sprinkle lightly with grated Parmesan. (If you have extra filling, coat a small dish with non-stick spray and bake it with the others; it's good cold.)

Bake at 375 F (190 C) for about 30 minutes, or until firm in the center. Let pies rest in the tins for about 5 minutes before removing.

Hash Brown Variation: In a pinch, frozen hash brown potatoes may be substituted for grated raw potatoes, cup for cup. The dish can also be baked as one large pie or as a somewhat thinner cake (using a 9 x 13 inch or 22 x 33 cm cake pan) by increasing the baking time to about an hour for a pie, 45 minutes for the thinner cake. The cake may be cut into small squares and served cold as an appetizer.

Spinach-Wrapped Cheese Grill

Bundles of spinach-wrapped cheese, spiked with jalapeno peppers and grilled until the greens are slightly toasted and the cheese is warm and melting, is a lovely prelude to a long, conversational night around the table with some interesting wines.

Although large spinach leaves are used in this recipe, almost any soft green will work: romaine, beet greens, chard, or vine leaves. If you haven't enough of one variety of green, or if you're in a mood for novelty, use a combination. Use any cheese that appeals to you, such as snow goat cheese or smoked mozzarella, or a combination of two cheeses, one on top of the other.

Serve the bundles on small plates with slices of toasted baguette. *Serves 6*

24	large spinach leaves	24
6	small fresh goat cheeses or 6 squares of other cheese	6
6 tsp	canned jalapenos, minced olive oil	30 mL

☐ Blanch the leaves in hot water for a few seconds, just until pliable. Pat dry. If using brined vine leaves, rinse and pat dry.

Lay the leaves on a cutting board, using 4 leaves per package. Center one cheese on each pile of leaves. Top with minced jalapenos. Wrap the leaves around the cheese, being sure to cover it completely. Tie with kitchen string and brush each bundle with olive oil.

Grill about 5 minutes per side. Snip string before serving.

Chapter 32 ■ *Tomatoes*

WHEN IT CAME TO TOMATOES, GRANDMA WAS A PURIST. SHE ATE FRESH tomatoes only in season, those few weeks of high summer when the days were still longish and the sun was hot enough to wilt the vines.

On a certain day in August, around noon, she'd stroll into her garden to the special tomato, the one she'd propped up with a shingle because it was so juice-heavy it was cracking the vine. If the moment was right, she'd pick it, dust it on her apron, and take the first bite right there with the sun feeling good on her face and the warm, sweet juice trickling down her throat. She knew that mortal meals didn't get much better than that.

Her tomatoes had names like Fireball and Starfire, and the funny one – Burpee. Their skin was taut over red, juicy flesh, and it was fragile and almost transparent, so it had to be handled with love. Some of her tomatoes had odd shapes, segmented like miniature pumpkins or rounded and plummy, with a tear-drop end. All of them were fleshy and juicy right through the middle, sweet in the mouth, with a fine acid edge to their flavor, so after the third bite, a pinch of salt seemed like a good idea.

After that first big tomato, grandma's plant still had six or seven pounds of fruit on the way. There were thick slabs of Beefsteaks, fried in butter and finished with cream, and there were chunks of slightly underripe Starfire, drizzled with good olive oil and a splash of vinegar, with a pinch of sugar and a handful of basil leaves chopped over top. When fresh tomatoes palled and frost threatened, there was a whole sweet pot of chili sauce blip-blipping on the stove and spicy green tomato pickles. You could smell the cloves and cinnamon from the front door. Finally, there was a cardboard box in a dark closet, and layers of newspaper and . . . the neighbors.

The rest of the year, she ate canned tomatoes because they were okay for soups, stews, and sauces, and North America hadn't yet cut back on salt and sugar in its diet so the nuances of tin in canned tomatoes didn't bother her. (So accustomed have we become to that hint of tin that one survey actually found that people preferred tin-canned tomatoes to the ones in glass jars.)

Tinny or not, one of her best winter dishes was cream of tomato soup made with canned tomatoes and milk, with a handful of salty soda crackers crumbled into it and stirred around until they were mushy. It was a comforting dish on a cold night.

The Tomato in History

Tomatoes have an enchanting history. Nobody had to convince the Italians what a treasure they had in the tomato. Always perceptive in matters of love, beauty, and food, they gave it a wonderful name, _pomo d'oro_ (the golden apple), and cherished it in their kitchens ever after.

For some reason, it took the French longer to see the light. They thought the tomato was a pretty plant and used it as an ornamental in their gardens, but they were terrified of eating it because it belonged to the deadly nightshade family. They named the tomato the _pomme d'amour_ because it was beautiful, mysterious, and forbidden – all the ingredients guaranteed to stir passion in the hearts of red-blooded Frenchmen.

And then, having adored it, they proceeded to let the fruit die on the vine.

Fortunately, along came Catherine de Medici, the young Florentine princess with the world's largest recipe file. When she married the French king, she insisted on hauling her entire kitchen and most of her cooks along to France, and soon – _eh, voilà!_ The French were mad about tomatoes.

The tomato probably reached North America via that great green thumb, Thomas Jefferson, who called it a Spanish cantaloupe. Although he is supposed to have stood on the steps of an important building bravely eating a tomato to prove to the assembled doubters that it was a perfectly safe thing to do, at least one historian insists that Jefferson did not eat that tomato because he was afraid of its deadly reputation. Yet another historian says he _did_ eat the tomato and loved it.

The truth? Avid trencherman that Jefferson was, he likely had a chat with his insurance agent and then pigged out.

So many anthems of praise have been written about the sun-ripened tomato that I hesitate to add another tune, but when the season rolls around and I pinch a leaf and that musty-spicy essence of tomato tickles my nose, I'm thrilled all over again.

from The Garden

The Plight of the Contemporary Tomato

Meanwhile, profit-wise commercial tomato growers in Mexico, California, and Florida have been applauding the development of the contemporary tomato, a handy item that defies time, season, or harvesting machines. It has a plastic skin, a hard, stringy core, and if you drop it, it'll bounce like a rubber ball. If picked when totally green and hard, it's virtually unsquashable.

True, it lacks those qualities usually associated with tomatoes: juice, flavor, texture, color, a certain easily-bruised fragility, but it makes up for these puny shortcomings in economy and efficiency. Too green to tempt you? A good shot of ethylene gas will turn it red in no time. Of course it will still taste green, but it'll look pretty, and as Calvin Trillin says, "its shelf life is approximately that of a mop handle."

With each passing year, I'm freshly appalled at what's been done in the name of tomato research. Fortunately, in spite of all attempts to force the tomato to grow bigger, faster, more prolific, and to develop a handy squared shape (the better to fit a packing tube) and a Methuselean shelf life, the tomato has not entirely conformed, and you can still grow a good one in any patch of earth with lots of sunlight, a little TLC, and enough water.

The trouble with re-inventing the tomato is that people tend to forget what it was all about in the first place. I once read in a respected food magazine that tomatoes for sandwiches should be peeled, seeded, chopped, and squeezed to rid them of excess juice. So why bother with a tomato? Why not a nice piece of styrofoam?

The way to make a tomato sandwich is with an honest tomato, one that's been left on the vine to ripen and has never seen the inside of a refrigerator. Slice it into thick slabs. Arrange the slices on good, crusty bread, generously buttered. Pinch of salt. Speck of pepper. Repeat the bread. Now *that's* a tomato sandwich.

A Parisian food writer summed up the dilemma of the contemporary tomato.

"This tomato is meaningless in the mouth," he fretted. "It is a vegetable that will lose its clientele."

Right. It's not good to mess with perfection.

IN THE MARKET: Ninety-five percent of the average tomato is water, but it's the other five percent that makes the difference, being evenly divided between sugars and acids: malic (think of apples) and citric (think of oranges.) There are about 400 other elements that combine to make up a tomato: vitamins, minerals, and those strange, magical grace notes we call volatile essences. The fine balance of flavors and textures we associate with tomato perfection depends on them.

Nearly 200 varieties of tomatoes are grown in North America, falling roughly into the categories of slicers for table use, beefsteaks (huge and juicy, with lots of jelly-like locular tissue), plum (a paste-type with a lot of firm, pericap tissue), and midget, commonly known as cherry tomatoes. Beyond these is a whole range of novelty tomatoes, a cornucopia of sizes, shapes, and colors. Flat or pear-shaped, yellow to green to blue-purple, often hollow and frequently juiceless, they are, in any event, novel.

The best tomato is the one in your own garden. Failing that, a market garden or farm stand in August is the place for summer tomatoes, especially if you find a grower who is a tomato enthusiast. Italian plum tomatoes such as La Rossa or Milano are your best bet for sauces, paste, or sun-drying. An odd looking plum tomato with a curved bottom known as the Super Italian Paste has a brown-sugary sweetness and cooks into a rich, red sauce. Among the beefsteak slicers, Dona, a new French hybrid, is sweet and juicy with beautifully balanced flavor.

Small, cherry-type tomatoes are perfect for salads and have wonderfully concentrated flavor when they aren't mass-produced. The smaller they are, the sassier they taste. I recently sampled a tiny, cranberry-sized tomato that looked positively insignificant, but what flavor!

The yellow tomatoes are milder and tend to have less acid than their red cousins. Although I'd hate to see them replace the traditional red model, they add interest to salads, and varieties such as Yellow Marble, Persimmon, and the flavorful, baseball-sized Taxi, are wowing tomato lovers.

■ **Nutrition:** The tomato is high in vitamin C, and is a good source of potassium, vitamin A, and phosphorus. One large, raw tomato has about 40 calories

■ **Season:** July through September, or until a killing frost.

■ **Buy:** Allow 1 medium tomato per person. It will yield about 3/4 cup (175 mL), coarsely chopped.

IN THE KITCHEN: Store stem end down at room temperature until ready to eat. Whatever variety you buy, do not refrigerate unless the tomatoes are already overripe. Once a tomato is cooled below 50 F (10 C), the flavor is virtually chilled out and the texture turns cottony.

For how to peel tomatoes, see note immediately before the recipes.

Cherry Tomatoes with Scented Basil

Peeling these tiny tomatoes takes a bit of patience, but the results are worth it. For the most concentrated flavor, use the smallest red cherry tomatoes you can find or a combination of red and yellow cherries or yellow pear tomatoes. If you're making the salad at the end of the season when the acid seems to drop off, leaving them sweet but bland, you may want a touch more vinegar.

I like to use one of the traditional Genoa-style basils with glossy, pointed leaves and a rich, heady perfume, or even lemon basil if you can get your hands on some. Cinnamon basil is also excellent in this dish, rounding and warming the flavors.

Serve these with any grilled meat or a whole, barbecued salmon.

Serves 6

4 cups	cherry tomatoes	1 L
1 tbsp	balsamic vinegar	15 mL
1/2 tsp	dry mustard	2 mL
1/4 cup	fresh lemon juice	50 mL
1/2 cup	olive oil	125 mL
1/2 cup	freshly shredded basil leaves	125 mL
	salt and freshly ground black pepper	

☐ Place tomatoes in a bowl and pour boiling water over them, testing after 40 seconds to see if the skins are loosening. Peel tomatoes and lay them in a flat container.

Whisk together the remaining ingredients. Pour the mixture over the peeled tomatoes and roll them around, tossing gently so the marinade touches every part of them.

Cover and marinate 2 hours before serving. If you must wait longer, this is the time to refrigerate tomatoes.

Baked Cherry Tomatoes

In the winter, cherry tomatoes baked with garlic, parsley, and buttery bread crumbs are a savory addition to roasted chicken. It's an old combination from southern France that loses nothing when used with smaller tomatoes, which needn't be peeled and take only moments to heat through.

For the bread crumbs, use a coarse-crumbed, multi-grain loaf.

Check the garlic to see if it has a green sprout in the center as often happens in winter. With the point of a paring knife, remove the green sprout as it will be bitter.

Serves 4

2 tsp	extra-virgin olive oil	10 mL
2 tsp	butter	10 mL
1 cup	fresh bread crumbs	250 mL
1	large clove garlic, pressed	1
1/2 cup	freshly minced parsley leaves, packed	125 mL
4 cups	cherry tomatoes	1 L
	salt and freshly ground black pepper	

☐ In a large frying pan, heat olive oil and butter together until butter foams.

Add bread crumbs and stir, letting them brown slightly.

Add garlic and minced parsley, and stir until hot.

Place tomatoes in a single layer in a well-buttered casserole or gratin dish. Sprinkle with the buttered crumbs. Season with salt and freshly ground pepper, and bake at 450 F (230 C) for about 10 minutes, or until the tomatoes just begin to split their skins. Serve immediately.

Salsa Cruda with Lime

There are some excellent salsas in a variety of strengths available in any supermarket. Still, there's nothing quite like a freshly made *salsa cruda* eaten with crisp corn chips.

If you want the extra flavor, here it is. Leftovers can be frozen in small plastic bags and thawed as needed.

Use jalapeno or serrano chilies, or even guero chilies if you can find them. The amount of heat you want in this sauce can be adjusted – just use more or less chili. The defining herbs, oregano and cilantro, should be adjusted to suit your own taste, and the cilantro should be coarsely chopped, not minced.

Makes about 4 cups (1 L)

3 to 5	small, hot chilies	3 to 5
1	small red bell pepper	1
1	small yellow bell pepper	1
1	sweet red onion	1
6	medium tomatoes	6
2	cloves garlic, pressed	2
1 tsp	dried oregano	5 mL
1/4 cup	cilantro, coarsely chopped	50 mL
1/2 tsp	grated lime zest	2 mL
	juice of 1 large lime	
1 tsp	salt	5 mL

☐ Finely mince the chilies, handling them as directed.

Mince the bell peppers and red onion.

Cut the tomatoes in fine dice. No need to peel.

Put chilies, peppers, and tomatoes in a non-metal bowl with onion, garlic, oregano, and cilantro.

Add lime zest, lime juice, and salt. Cover the salsa and refrigerate overnight for flavors to mellow. This can be frozen in small containers.

Gratin of Tomatoes with Garlic Cream

Such a simple dish, this. Yet it's a celebration of freshness and flavor – a summer dish that is only possible when tomatoes are at their peak. It makes a small supper for two.

Don't be tempted to overdo the garlic here – it's the grace note, not the whole tune. The cream is simmered to reduce it slightly and give it a silken texture. It's important to make the croutons at the last minute so they're crisp and hot.

Serves 2

1	small clove garlic	1
3/4 cup	cream	75 mL
	salt and freshly ground pepper	
2	large field tomatoes, sliced	2
1/4 cup	freshly grated Parmesan cheese	50 mL
3	slices multi-grain bread	3

☐ Slice garlic clove in half and place in a small saucepan with the cream.

Bring to a boil, reduce heat to a simmer, and cook about 6 minutes, or until slightly reduced. Scoop out the garlic and discard. Add salt sparingly and grind in some black pepper.

Butter a small gratin dish and lay the tomato slices in it. Drizzle with cream and sprinkle with grated Parmesan cheese. Bake at 450 F (230 C) for about 10 minutes.

Meanwhile, cut bread slices into six pieces each, trimming off the crusts. Place on an ungreased pan and bake in the same oven until crisp and golden-brown, turning once.

Distribute hot croutons between two soup plates. Serve tomatoes and sauce over top.

Oven-Grilled Tomatoes with Buffala and Basil

Another exquisitely simple dish, this one requires the best ingredients: soft, fresh buffala cheese from a good Italian deli, highly-scented Genoa-type basil leaves, and meaty beefsteak tomatoes that are dead-ripe.

Serves 4

1 lb	buffala cheese	500 g
1	crisp baguette, halved lengthwise	1
	fresh basil leaves	
2 or 3	large beefsteak tomatoes, peeled	2 or 3
	extra-virgin olive oil	
	salt and pepper	

☐ Turn oven to broil.

Slice the buffala and lay on the bread halves, covering the bread completely.

Reserving several of the best leaves for garnish, mince about 1/2 cup (125 mL) of basil leaves and sprinkle generously over the cheese.

Slice the tomatoes and lay them, overlapping, on the cheese. Sprinkle a few drops of olive oil on the tomatoes, but don't drown them; there should be a mere hint of oil.

Season lightly with salt and pepper.

Place on a cookie sheet and broil, 8 inches (20 cm) from the grill, until tomatoes pucker slightly and cheese begins to melt and bubble. Serve hot, garnished with fresh basil leaves.

Sweet Tomato Chutney

Back when people canned hundreds of jars of any vegetable that crossed their path, tomato chutney was a big hit. It's still one of the best of the easy fall pickles. This one is sweet and spicy, and it enhances everything from grilled meats to cold leftover roasts to pureed squash.

Makes about 6 cups (1 1/2 L)

12	medium tomatoes, peeled and coarsely chopped	12
2	large onions, chopped	2
2	stalks celery, diced	2
2	green bell peppers, chopped	2
2	jalapeno peppers, finely minced	2
1 cup	golden raisins	250 mL
1 cup	sugar	250 mL
1 tbsp	salt	15 mL
1 1/2 cups	cider vinegar	375 mL
2 tsp	cinnamon	10 mL
2 tsp	allspice	10 mL
1 tsp	mustard seed	5 mL
1 tsp	celery seed	5 mL

☐ Put all ingredients in a heavy kettle. Bring to a boil, reduce heat to simmer, and cook gently for about 2 hours, stirring often to be sure it doesn't burn. When thickened, pour into small, sterilized jars and seal. Store in refrigerator. This will keep several months.

Tomato Onion Tart, Provençal Style

This is one of the most versatile and satisfying dishes to serve, either as an appetizer with a glass of wine or as part of a brunch. Once you have mastered the simple task of rolling and baking the puff pastry, you can vary the vegetables almost at will.

Although this looks best when baked blind before filling, some cooks will simply not bother, and their pastry will be slightly puffed and irregular but delicious nonetheless.

Makes 8 large squares, 32 small

1/2	14.5 oz (411 g) pkg puff pastry	1/2
1/4 cup	mayonnaise	50 mL
1 tbsp	butter	15 mL
2	large onions, chopped	2
3	eggs	3
1/2 cup	whipping cream	250 mL
1 cup	Gruyère cheese, grated	250 mL
3 tsp	fresh parsley, minced	15 mL
5 or 6	large ripe tomatoes, peeled	5 or 6
	salt and freshly ground pepper	

☐ Thaw puff pastry according to package directions.

Preheat oven to 400 F (200 C).

Roll pastry on a lightly floured board to a rectangle that will fit your cookie sheet. Roll it back over the rolling pin and transfer to the sheet, patting it around the edges to form a lip. Crimp the edges. Prick the surface all over with a fork.

Lay a sheet of aluminum foil on the pastry and fill it with dried beans or baking weights (tiny metal beans that can be purchased in specialty stores for baking pastry blind.) Bake the pastry at 400 F (200 C), about 12 minutes.

Remove from oven, remove weights and foil, and brush pastry with mayonnaise.

In a large frying pan, melt the butter. Sauté onions until transparent, using a slotted spoon to transfer to a bowl to cool.

Beat together eggs, cream, and half the cheese. Stir in the onions. Pour evenly into the pastry. Sprinkle with parsley. Slice tomatoes thinly and lay over the onions, overlapping slightly. Sprinkle with salt, pepper, and the remaining cheese. Bake at 350 F (180 C) for 20 minutes. Serve warm or cold, cut in squares. Using a good pizza cutter will simplify the task.

Three Onion Variation: Instead of using tomatoes, double the amount of onions using a combination of yellow and red onions and a few chopped green ones for color and texture. Proceed as above.

Tomato Salad with Warm Balsamic Vinegar and Bacon

When winter shuts down the garden and tomatoes are less than pristine, this hot vinaigrette brings out hidden flavors and enhances them. The addition of balsamic vinegar balances the richness of bacon fat and gives it the warm flavor these winter tomatoes need.

Serves 4

4	tomatoes, sliced thickly	4
4	slices bacon, diced	4
1	small onion, minced	1
1/4 cup	red wine vinegar	50 mL
1 tbsp	balsamic vinegar	15 mL
1 tbsp	brown sugar	15 mL
	black pepper	

☐ Arrange tomatoes on a dark-colored platter – black or marine blue makes a stunning background for the red tomatoes.

Fry bacon and onion together until onion is transparent and bacon fat is mostly rendered.

Pour vinegars into the pan and sprinkle with sugar. As soon as it simmers, pour it over the sliced tomatoes.

Add a few turns from the pepper mill and serve at once with toasted baguette slices and a nippy Cheddar cheese.

Tomato Pudding

Essentially a winter dish, this gently spicy concoction often appeared for Monday lunch when my grandmother was in charge of the kitchen. I was fascinated to find a similar dish in Italy, served as a soup, and made there, as it was in our home kitchen, with canned tomatoes. Grandma used her own home-canned tomatoes, but any good brand of Italian plum tomatoes will do. Tomato pudding is homey stuff, good with meat loaf and baked potatoes.

Serves 6

4 cups	canned tomatoes with juice	1 L
1/4 tsp	cinnamon	1 mL
1 tsp	vinegar	5 mL
1/2 tsp	pepper	2 mL
1 tsp	salt or to taste	5 mL
1/4 cup	brown sugar, packed	50 mL
1	small onion, finely diced	1
1 tbsp	butter	15 mL
6	slices bread, cut in small cubes	6
	Parmesan cheese *(optional)*	

☐ Preheat oven to 400 F (200 C).

In a large measuring cup or medium bowl, stir together the tomatoes, spices, vinegar, salt, pepper, and brown sugar.

Melt the butter in a small pan and fry the onion until transparent but not browned. Place bread cubes in a well-buttered 6 cup (1.5 L) casserole and pour onions and melted butter over them. Pour tomato mixture over top. Bake for about 50 minutes.

This is sprinkled with Parmesan cheese in Italy, but in Saskatchewan that would have been a sinful extravagance. I say, follow your own conscience and pass the Parmesan.

Tomato Focaccia with Tomato, Garlic, and Parmesan

On a summer afternoon, the delicious combination of freshly baked flatbread and ripe tomatoes makes this simple dish one of my all-time favorite lunches. The crust of the bread is brushed with garlic-infused olive oil, then sprinkled with a few fresh oregano leaves, finely minced. If you haven't any garlic oil on hand, just brush the bread with olive oil and rub it with a cut clove of garlic.

Serve it with Artichokes in Pesto Cream with Tomatoes and Olives (see section on Artichokes for recipe), and you'll have a wonderful lunch. If you're picnicking, pack the tomatoes in a separate container and add just before eating.

Serves 6 as an appetizer, 4 as lunch main course

1	loaf Focaccia with Summer Herbs (see section on Herbs for recipe)	1
	garlic-infused olive oil	
4 or 5	large, meaty tomatoes	4 or 5
1/4 cup	fresh parsley, minced	50 mL
1 tbsp	balsamic vinegar	15 mL
	fresh oregano leaves, chopped, or dry oregano to taste	
	salt and coarsely ground black pepper	
	fresh oregano or chives, garnish	

☐ Brush top of cooked loaf with garlic oil. Peel and dice tomatoes into a medium bowl. Add parsley, vinegar, oregano, salt, and pepper. Toss. Cut focaccia into wedges and pile generously with tomatoes. Serve cold or heat briefly in oven. Garnish with sprigs of fresh oregano or wisps of chive.

Cheese and Black Olive Variation: If you're using the plain herbed focaccia made without cheese, add a few ripe olives, roughly chopped, and a good smash of grated Asiago or Parmesan to the tomato mixture and broil until heated through. This is also a good topping for toasted baguette slices that have been brushed with garlic-infused oil.

Chapter 33 ■ Turnips and Rutabagas

EVERYBODY IN OUR HOUSE LOVED TURNIPS, OR WHAT WE CALLED turnips. Imagine my surprise when they turned out to be rutabagas.

I grew up calling rutabagas turnips and ignoring real turnips because they were small, bitter, and weepy, and nobody in my household grew them. I eventually learned to like them during a year with some Hungarian nuns who were as poor as they were pious and cooked whatever came to the kitchen door, including free turnips. They were inclined to boil them, mash them with a lot of butter and freshly grated nutmeg, and stir in a dollop of sour cream. I've also enjoyed small turnips roasted around a nice fat duckling.

I cannot improve on either method, but my firm advice is to avoid any turnip bigger than a large radish. The smaller ones are sweet and crisp, but as they grow, they tend to go woody, stringy, and bitter.

In the Market: Look for the French varieties such as De Nancy, which are sweet, creamy fleshed, and mild, or the small, early Market Express.

Rutabagas are another matter. They take twice as long to grow and thrive in cold climates. Laurentian is a reliable variety, and after the first frost has touched it, this is a naturally sweet, golden vegetable that flavors stews and soups all winter long.

■ ***Nutrition:*** Good to excellent source of vitamin C, good source of iron and potassium, and high in fiber. One cup (250 mL) of cooked rutabaga has about 36 calories.

■ ***Season:*** Late fall, after the first frost has sweetened them, through early spring.

■ ***Buy:*** 1 medium rutabaga serves 4; 1 small to medium turnip serves 1.

IN THE KITCHEN: Turnips and rutabagas are obliging vegetables, taking nicely to almost any cooking method you feel like trying. They're good raw, either cut into sticks and served with a dip or grated into a salad. They can be steamed, boiled, microwaved, or stir-fried with equal success.

A wisp of sugar enhances the flavor of cooked, mashed turnips as does a squirt of lemon juice or a little freshly grated nutmeg.

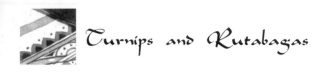

Rutabaga with Bacon and Sautéed Apple

The wisp of cinnamon and nutmeg is so subtle that you'll hardly notice it, yet it compliments the sweet qualities of the rutabaga and rounds off the sharp edges.

Serves 6

3 cups	diced rutabaga	750 mL
3	slices side bacon, diced	3
1	small onion, diced	1
1	large apple, peeled and diced	1
1/4 cup	brown sugar	50 mL
1/4 tsp ea	cinnamon and nutmeg	1 mL ea
	salt and pepper	

☐ In a medium pot, cover rutabaga with water and bring to a boil. Cook until tender. Drain.

In a large frying pan, cook bacon until nearly crisp. Add onion and apple, and stir-fry in bacon fat until onion is transparent. Sprinkle with sugar. Add rutabaga and stir-fry briefly, seasoning with cinnamon, nutmeg, salt, and pepper. Serve hot.

Rutabaga with Honey and Soy Sauce

Again, a touch of sweetness enlivens a simple vegetable.

Serves 6

4 cups	rutabaga, slivered	1 L
1	medium carrot, slivered	1
1/2 cup	water	125 mL)
1 tbsp	butter	15 mL
1 tbsp	honey	15 mL
1 tbsp	soy sauce	15 mL
1 tbsp	lemon juice	15 mL
	salt and pepper	

☐ Place vegetables in a broad, flat pan with water, butter, honey, soy sauce, and lemon juice. Bring to a boil and cook, uncovered, until nicely glazed.

Reduce heat and continue cooking until tender, adding a little water if it threatens to dry out. The vegetables should be lightly browned and almost candied.

Season with salt and pepper.

Rutabaga Potato Fry-Up

The day after Christmas, this dish always appeared at suppertime with cold turkey, hot gravy, and leftover stuffing. The potatoes seemed to cushion the rather strident rutabaga, which grew sweeter in combination. Do let this brown a little on the bottom. The crusty bits are delicious.

Serves 6

1 tbsp	canola oil	15 mL
1 tbsp	butter	15 mL
1	small onion, diced	1
2 cups	leftover mashed rutabagas	500 mL
2 cups	leftover mashed potatoes	500 mL
	salt and pepper	

☐ In a large frying pan, heat oil and butter until foamy. Add onion and stir fry quickly.

Add rutabaga and potatoes, breaking them up and stirring them into one another. Season with salt and pepper, and cook over low heat until hot through and the bottom has just begun to brown.

Spoon into a serving bowl. Serve with turkey gravy.

Rutabaga Patty Variation: If you love the crusty part of this dish, mix the onion, potato, and rutabaga together in a large bowl and beat in an egg. Dust with flour. Form into patties and sauté in hot butter, turning once. Keep hot and serve with Sweet Tomato Chutney (see section on Tomatoes for recipe).

Gratin of Turnips and Potatoes in Cream

By now you've probably noticed my fondness for gratins, but they are, in a northern climate, among the most satisfying ways to cook root vegetables during the colder months. The long, slow cooking takes full advantage of stored flavors and brings out their best qualities.

Serves 8 to 10

3 tbsp	butter	45 mL
2 cups	half-and-half cream	500 mL
3	cloves garlic, pressed	3
4	large potatoes, thinly sliced	4
1	small rutabaga or 4 small turnips, thinly sliced	1
	salt, pepper, and freshly grated nutmeg	
1/2 cup	grated Gruyère or Asiago cheese	125 mL

☐ Preheat oven to 400 F (200 C).

Lavishly butter a 9 x 13 inch (4 L) baking dish.

In a small pot, heat cream to just below boiling. Stir in the pressed garlic.

Alternately layer thinly sliced potatoes and rutabagas or turnips in the buttered dish. Lightly season each layer of potatoes with salt and pepper, and add a wisp of freshly grated nutmeg to the turnip layers. (Be judicious here – fresh nutmeg is powerful.) Pour hot garlic cream over the vegetables. Sprinkle with freshly grated cheese.

Bake 20 minutes at 400 F (200 C). Reduce heat to 350 F (180 C) and continue baking another 35 to 40 minutes, or until vegetables are tender. Add a little milk during baking if the vegetables appear to be drying out; this should be a creamy dish.

When vegetables are softly tender, remove from oven and let rest about 10 minutes.

Chapter 34 ■ Zucchini

When I was writing this book and got all the way to zucchini, I thought I was nearly finished and said so.

"But zucchini goes on forever," said my friend Mitch, prophetically.

Too true.

Zucchini, reliably prolific, has spawned no end of recipes, from the sublime to the ridiculous. Zucchini chocolate cake? Yes. Zucchini ice cream?

Help, we're over the edge.

IN THE MARKET: There are a passle of new varieties of summer squash coming into the markets, and although the long, green Italian (known in French cookbooks as the *courgette*) is still the most popular all-around summer squash, the pale green Lebanese Cousa, the long Golden Zucchini, Yellow Crookneck, and Sunburst (a type of pattypan that has a beautiful golden yellow skin) are gaining acceptance, too. In early summer, it's now possible to find the ultimate luxury – baby zucchini with blossoms attached, and occasionally, the paler green, golf-ball sized zucchini known as Global, also with blossom attached.

Look for small to medium-sized zucchini with smooth, unbroken skin. The glossier it is, the more recently it has been picked.

■ *Nutrition:* High in vitamin C and fiber; low in calories, about 25 per cup (250 mL), cooked.

■ *Season:* June through October

■ *Buy:* 1 small zucchini, about 4 oz (115 g) per person.

IN THE KITCHEN: Don't wash zucchini until you're ready to cook with it, as the skin is extremely tender and bruises easily. It will keep in the refrigerator, in plastic, for up to 5 days.

*Zucchini Lime
Tea Bread with
Lime Glaze*

from The Garden

When cooking zucchini or other summer squash, there's no need to peel unless it's overmature, in which case you're better off to donate it to the compost pile.

Zucchini can be sliced crosswise or lengthwise, or halved, hollowed, and stuffed. It goes well in omelets and frittatas, stir-fries, ratatouille, or as part of almost any meat-based casserole. It has a special affinity for garlic and tomatoes.

In fact, most cooks have more zucchini recipes than they know what to do with. Here's one (and only one) more.

Zucchini Lime Tea Bread with Lime Glaze

A pale, tender bread flecked with green and spiked with fresh lime, this is one of my favorites. It's especially delicious served with a perfect cup of tea.

Makes 1 loaf

2 cups	zucchini, grated and packed	500 mL
	juice and zest of 1 large lime	
2 cups	all-purpose flour	500 mL
1/2 tsp	salt	2 mL
1/2 tsp	baking soda	2 mL
2 tsp	baking powder	10 mL
1/2 tsp	freshly grated nutmeg	2 mL
1 cup	sugar	250 mL
1	egg	1
1/2 cup	canola oil	125 mL
1/2 cup	plain yogurt	125 mL

☐ Preheat oven to 350 F (180 C). Coat a 9 x 5 inch (2 L) loaf pan with non-stick spray.

Put grated zucchini on a clean tea towel and wring to remove as much liquid as possible.

In a medium bowl, stir together all dry ingredients. Grate the lime peel. Add to dry ingredients.

Beat together the egg, oil, and yogurt. Squeeze lime juice and add to liquid. Make a well in dry ingredients and pour liquid into it.

Add grated zucchini. Stir together with a fork until just mixed – batter will be thick and lumpy. Spoon into loaf pan. Bake 55 to 60 minutes. Cool 10 minutes before turning out on a cake rack. With a toothpick, poke several holes in the loaf at intervals. While still warm, spoon the glaze over top.

Lime Glaze

1/2	cup icing sugar, sifted	125 mL
	juice of 1 lime	
1 tsp	finely grated lime zest	5 mL

☐ Put all ingredients in a measuring cup and stir to partly dissolve the sugar. If there isn't enough juice, add a few drops of water. Microwave the glaze just until it boils. Spoon glaze over the loaf. Chill before serving.

From The Garden

Index

from The Garden

from The Garden